The Treasure of PRAYER

The Treasure of PRAYER

UNDER THE DIRECTION OF
JACQUES PHILIPPE
AND ANNE OF JESUS (ED.)

From the same collection: *Prayer: Oxygen for Believers*, © Scepter Publishers, 2024.

Translated by Christian Lingua.
Unless otherwise stated, translations of quotes are ours.

Certain quotations may have been stylistically adjusted to ensure consistency throughout the text.

This English translation is published by Scepter Publishers, Inc.
info@scepterpublishers.org
www.scepterpublishers.org
800–322–8773
New York

Cover design: Marc Whitaker, MTW Design
Page design and composition: Christian Lingua

Library of Congress Control Number: 2024949391

ISBN paperback: 978–1–59417–544–2
ISBN eBook: 978–1–59417–545–9

Printed in the United States of America

Contents

Introduction

FR. JACQUES PHILIPPE

This book is a continuation of *Prayer: Oxygen for the Soul*, published in English in 2024. Much like the first publication, this is a collection of various writings concerning prayer and spiritual life, written by the brothers and sisters of the Community of the Beatitudes. These writings were initially created for members and friends of the Community, but now they have been made available to anyone searching for help and nourishment in their prayer journey.

This book is all the more timely because Pope Francis, when referring to the preparations for the Great Jubilee in 2025, had asked that 2024 be a year especially dedicated to prayer, like a

> great "symphony" of prayer. Prayer, above all else, to renew our desire to be in the presence of the Lord, to listen to him and to adore him. . . . Prayer that makes it possible for every man and woman in this

> world to turn to the one God and to reveal to him what lies hidden in the depths of their heart. Prayer as the royal road to holiness, which enables us to be contemplative even in the midst of activity.[1]

Through the voice of the Pope, and also through all of the difficult challenges our world must face today, The Holy Spirit is clearly asking us for a real outcry of prayer. It is of vital importance that people turn their hearts toward God, faithfully taking the time to be in his presence, receiving from him the very grace that allows us to always be hopeful, to grow in both faith and love, and to find the correct answers to the challenges we face in today's world.

Without the light and the strength that come from being with God in prayer, we are too weak to face our struggles alone. A Christian who does not pray is a Christian in danger, said Pope John Paul II in his apostolic exhortation *Novo millenio ineunte*, published at the beginning of the third millennium. A Christian who commits to communicating with God in prayer, both collectively and personally—even if the prayer is simple and lowly—will always have the grace necessary to live in a positive way, no matter what he is faced with.

---

1. Francis, Letter to Msgr. Rino Fisichella, President of the Pontifical Council for the Promotion of the New Evangelization, for the Jubilee 2025 (February 11, 2022). www.vatican.va.

We hope this book encourages readers on their beautiful journey of union with God, through Christ and in the Holy Spirit—a journey on which we are all called. May our perseverance in prayer allow us to "*taste and see that the Lord is good!*" (Ps 34:8), with the expectation that we will one day live together in fellowship with God and with one another in his kingdom.

1

Union with God

FR. JACQUES PHILIPPE

What God seeks, He being Himself God by nature, is to make us gods through participation, just as fire converts all things into fire.[1]

—St. John of the Cross

Our vocation: a union with God!

"*And I will betroth you to me for ever; I will betroth you to me in righteousness and in justice, in steadfast love, and in mercy. I will betroth you to me in faithfulness; and you shall know the Lord*" (Hos 2:19–20). Do we not want the promises of Scripture fulfilled for us? The ultimate goal of our mission is nothing less than a union with God.

---

1. John of the Cross, *Maxims and Counsels*, no. 28, in *The Collected Works of St. John of the Cross*, rev. ed., trans. Kieran Kavanaugh, OCD, and Otilio Rodriguez, OCD (ICS, 1973), p. 676, https://archive.org/details/collectedworksof0000unse_h3m3.

To know him intimately and to love him earnestly. Oh, how we are loved and known by God! We want to abide in him, as he abides in us (see Jn 15:4). We also want to be able to say, like St. Paul: "*I have been crucified with Christ; it is no longer I who live, but Christ who lives in me*" (Gal 2:20) so that, in St. Peter's words, we can "*become partakers of the divine nature*" (2 Pt 1:4). We want to live as if "*all mine are thine, and thine are mine, and I am glorified in them*" (Jn 17:10), in the way that is unique to the mutual gift of marriage between husband and wife, even if we must agree to the painful purification process which is necessary for this union; a union which itself requires a great purity of heart.

In addition to Scripture, the Carmelite tradition invites us to earnestly aspire to this aspect of Christian life; that of matrimony. The magnificent writings of St. John of the Cross describe the splendor of a soul transformed by God, and offer us a new outlook and an extraordinary hope:

> Besides teaching her [the soul] to love purely, freely, disinterestedly, as He loves her, God makes her love Him with the very strength with which He loves her. Transforming her into His own love . . . He gives her His own strength by which she can love Him.[2]

---

2. John of the Cross, *Spiritual Canticle*, in *Collected Works*, p. 554.

The soul in this state is much like the bride who has entered the bridal chamber of her bridegroom and is united with him in perfect love.

Union with God: a sensitive experience?

A union with God can sometimes be experienced to a significant degree, echoing through the various aspects of a person (igniting the will, filling the memory, brightening the intelligence, delighting the emotions and even the body). This allows us to experience a level of joy, happiness, and fullness that infinitely surpasses anything that the world can offer. But this is not always the case. Christian life on earth often consists of the desires and expectations of the spouse, and not only the spouse as a possession. Above all, this desire is expressed and is kept alive through a commitment to prayer.

We understand that the essence of a union does not lie purely in the emotions but is also a union of our will with his: a desire for nothing else except what God wants for us. He who with faith can accept poverty, darkness, and suffering can be more united with God than he who enjoys great riches. We can sometimes have obligations that demand our full attention and do not give us much time to consider God or to be in his presence. When this happens, we are not driven by these obligations, but we are instead filled with humility and faithfulness. In this way, we are deeply united with God, because we are simply doing what he expects of us. As the Carmelite saint Thérèse of Lisieux teaches us, the monotony of our sacrifice unites us more firmly with God than the bliss of ecstasy.

The more faith, hope, and love that a soul possesses, the more united this soul is with God. This is the basic teaching of St. John of the Cross. But as we all know, we are sometimes called to believe without seeing, to hope without possessing, and to love without satisfaction.

Can you measure your union with God?

It is difficult to measure one's union with God. Many saints have experienced a deeply profound union with God, yet at the same time have had feelings of extreme inner poverty. This was the case for Thérèse of Lisieux in her final years on this earth, as it was for Mother Teresa of Calcutta. Even if a union with God is both real and profound, it does not always bring joy to one's soul; a person can sometimes experience periods of great darkness and can feel more like he belongs "at the table of sinners" than in the hallways of heaven. The Lord allows his faithful servants to feel the weight of the world's sin on their shoulders. This is experienced as a mysterious type of solidarity, and seems to be a frequent occurrence today. If there are any criteria for measuring a person's union with God, they certainly will not be found in human senses and emotions. Instead, the most reliable criteria are how humble a person is, how attentive and charitable the person is toward the people in his life, and how peacefully and trustingly he accepts anything that may come his way, including disappointment and suffering. Acceptance of the cross is the most effective way to put us on the path toward a union with God.

Although no one can measure their union with God, we know with certainty how to achieve it: Having commitment to prayer, poverty of heart, humility, patience, gentleness, humble service, purity of heart, mercy, peace—this is what the Beatitudes practiced. There is no other way to the kingdom of God than this.

Seeing God in everything

Here is a passage from a letter written by Fr. Marie-Étienne Vayssière to one of his companions:

> Pursue a union with God relentlessly. How can you do this? By dying to yourself, by purifying your inner self, through humility, gentleness, patience, denial of self, a generous lack of focus on the self,

> and unreservedly abandoning the self. Sing God's will in all details that arise beneath your feet at any given moment. Be a faithful soul that sees God in everything, in his will and in his love, following his will unreservedly with an eternal impulse of the heart. In essence, all is to be found in a life of faith: all sanctification and all virtue. See God in everything. God and his infinite love are even found in the specks of dust we trample, in the hairs that fall from our heads, and in the leaves that move. Respond to this love of God with adherence and love in our hearts. Be joyful and content with everything, as everything is from God, therefore everything is God. Make this the great principle of your spiritual life, the true foundation on which you rest. Your journey forward will be filled with safety, speed, joy and fruitfulness of spirit.[3]

There are other aspects in the union with God to expand upon. With the works of Teresa of Ávila, we know that the foundation of a union with God is the mystery of the Incarnation, and that a union with God is achieved through a loving fellowship with the humanity of Jesus Christ. With the works of St. Louis-Marie Grignion de Montfort, we know that

---

3. Marie-Étienne Vayssière, *Consentir à l'amour: Lettres choisies* (Éditions des Béatitudes, 2018), p. 127.

Mary plays an essential role in leading us toward this. But we can't go into great detail here.

Walking toward God

In summation, let us find encouragement and inspiration in this beautiful passage by Fr. Vayssière:

> The soul that prays, no matter what its hardships, is always moving towards God. And the hardships that seem to delay its journey only hasten it. It is not the feeling we have of God that unites us to him, but rather the feeling of our despair, and, in this despair lies the confidence that uplifts us and pushes us forward despite everything. Carry out your daily spiritual exercises with humility. Walk continuously in this humility, in the knowledge that you are nothing and can do no good, but at the same time in boundless confidence in the infinite mercy of our heavenly Father.[4]

4. Vayssière, pp. 138–139.

Spiritual exercise

How much do I desire a union with God?

. . . .

. . . .

. . . .

. . . .

Is it my top priority in life?

. . . .

. . . .

. . . .

. . . .

Is it the thing I most yearn for?

. . . .

. . . .

. . . .

. . . .

Has my desire for this reduced over the years?

What could have reduced it?

Is it that my hardships in life have caused me disillusionment, discouragement, or loss of hope?

Do I intensely desire something other than God?

. . . .

. . . .

. . . .

. . . .

What steps can I take to reawaken this desire and keep it alive? (Consider these questions, knowing that they will be addressed in the following chapters.).

. . . .

. . . .

. . . .

. . . .

2

God's Desire

SR. MARIE-PASCALE

Let him kiss me with the kiss of his mouth. There is no question of ingratitude on my part, it is simply that I am in love. The favors I have received are far above what I deserve, but they are less than what I long for. It is desire that drives me on, not reason. Please do not accuse me of presumption if I yield to this impulse of love.[1]

—St. Bernard of Clairvaux

A mysterious desire

Man has many desires, but his greatest desire is a yearning for endless fulfillment, even if he can't give a name to this deep sense of longing. "Man carries within himself a mysterious desire for God."[2] "My *soul*

1. Bernard of Clairvaux, *On the Song of Songs I*, trans. Kilian Walsh, OCSO (Cistercian, 1981), Sermon 9, no. 2, p. 54, https://archive.org/details/onsongofsongs0000bern.

2. Benedict XVI, General Audience (November 7, 2012). www.vatican.va.

longs, yea, faints for the courts of the Lord; my heart and flesh sing for joy to the living God" (Ps 84:2). This desire moves us toward a yearning for that which is good.

"The desire for God is written in the human heart, because man is created by God and for God; and God never ceases to draw man to himself."[3] The bride in the Song of Songs says, *"I sought him whom my soul loves"* (Song 3:1). This desire engages a forward movement. *"But I press on to make it my own, because Christ Jesus has made me his own"* (Phil 3:12). It is also a type of martyrdom. St. Thérèse confesses that desire sometimes borders on martyrdom, like a fire that consumes you. She experienced this in prayer as she followed her mission in the heart of the Church.

Maintaining desire

Honeymoons don't last, but there comes a time for deep love to take root. The beloved is seeking a certain *je ne sais quoi* that the heart yearns to find, while being aware of how much this desire must be nurtured:

> For all the beauty man can gain
> Never my life away I'll fling,
> But rather for some other thing

---

3. *Catechism of the Catholic Church* 2nd ed. (Libreria Editrice Vaticana–United States Conference of Catholic Bishops, 2000), no. 27.

Which happy chance may well attain.[4]

Victory is achieved through seemingly small and insignificant things which are actually greatly important:

– these *words of love* fly from the heart like arrows to pierce the breast of the Beloved, which our heart alone chooses;

– the *love letter of Scripture* always feels new, no matter how many times you read it. Its verses are shocking and will shake you to your very foundations. You will immediately want to write them down in a little notebook;

– *gratitude* is a canvas for the soul to paint on. It is a blessing upon the world, which our neighbor the Church calls us to express;

– the *desire to be kind* to all people;

– the *law of giving*, following the example that Jesus set us; "*For the Son of man also came not to be served but to serve, and to give his life as a ransom for many*" (Mk 10:45);

– a *culture of trust* that liberates us: not everyone has an innate and ironclad trust in God like St. Thérèse did; my desire ends when I do not dare to believe that I

4. John of the Cross, "Ballad with a Divine Meaning," in *The Complete Works of Saint John of the Cross*, ed. E. Allison Peers, vol. 2 (Burns, Oates, & Washbourne, 1946), p. 468, https://schoolofmary.org/wp-content/uploads/2023/04/scribd.vpdfs_.com_the-complete-works-of-saint-john-of-the-cross-volume-2.pdf.

can please a God who is looking for *me*, a poor sinner;

– constant *purification* from sin, in reconciliation with God.

The risk of stifling desire

Desire can suppressed and can burn out, like a fire without air. How can this happen? Most often this happens through small, imperceptible changes which add up over time. Man's natural desire for knowledge is a normal expression of intelligence, and indeed a healthy level of curiosity is both praiseworthy and necessary. However, this runs counter to a fatal flaw; the increasing sole attraction to that which has been "created," and the mind's preoccupation with transient and useless knowledge, instead of knowledge of Scripture, which provides the soul with deep nourishment. Looking away from it is not beneficial to the soul.

So, what did the bride in the Song of Songs who suddenly refused to open her door do wrong? Seemingly nothing serious: She is coping fine without him and prefers an easy life, but "He who seeks God and yet wants his own satisfaction and rest, seeks Him at night and thus will not find him."[5] This is a type of *acedia*; a spiritual laziness that lies between sleep and cowardice.

5. John of the Cross, *Spiritual Canticle*, stanza 3, no. 3, in *Collected Works*, p. 429.

It is a lack of enthusiasm, which John Vianney, the Curé of Ars, describes as being *abominable*. The Church of Ephesus in the Apocalypse had lost the passion and drive of its first love: It became heavy, sad, and lacked enthusiasm. Neither hot nor cold, it had become lukewarm and indifferent, preferring instead to go along with the world's desires. It stopped setting itself apart or focusing on God's Word.

It's easy to over-invest yourself in things which can lead to a lack of desire for God. Here are two main examples:

Over-investment in work. Even with the best of intentions, or in the service of our mission for God, we can become addicted to our work. The founders, the saints, the great missionaries, Teresa of Ávila, François Régis, Mother Teresa, and so many others prayed at night; as did Pope Francis. It is vitally important to consciously make time to rest, have some essential breathing space and balance yourself; and also to recharge and spend some indispensable time in *lectio divina* and prayer. When you start to become aware that you are losing your drive and passion, it's good to pick up a book that stirs your soul. Everyone has their own book that has this effect on them. For example, Thérèse charismatically asked for a text from *The Imitation of Jesus Christ*. If you do not do this, however, you gradually lose your desire to seek out God, and you can become spiritually exhausted, sometimes to the point of burnout.

Emotional over-investment. Excessive emotional attachments, a heart divided between two desires, lack of freedom in the soul, suppression of emotions, numbing of emotions, and losing your desire for the Lord above. The sanctuary of the soul is no longer protected, and neither is the bridal chamber or the important time for a heart-to-heart with Christ and Christ alone, *ipsi soli*.

It's in our power to rekindle desire

"*Truly, thou art a God who hidest thyself, O God of Israel, the Savior*" (Is 45:15). When desire is lessened, surrounded by despair, or even gone completely, we feel helpless. Yet our desire (the Holy Spirit) still stirs within the depths of our being. He is waiting for what little goodwill we have within ourselves to reveal itself. Paul encouraged Timothy to rekindle the flame of desire: "*Hence I remind you to rekindle the gift of God that is within you through the laying on of my hands*" (2 Tm 1:6). We must work together with God in patience to rekindle our faith. The Holy Spirit helps us to overcome this spiritual laziness.

St. Augustine tells us that

> God, by deferring our hope, stretches our desire; by the desiring, stretches the mind; by stretching, makes it more capacious. . . . Suppose that God would fill you with honey: if you are full of vinegar, where will you put the honey? That which the vessel bore in it must be poured out: the vessel itself must be cleansed; must be cleansed, albeit with labor, albeit with hard rubbing, that it may become fit for that thing, whatever it be. Let us say honey, say gold, say wine; whatever we say it is, being that which cannot be said, whatever we would fain say, It is called—God.[6]

Mary's immense desire for God is what attracted the Word of God to her. As with Mary, we too long to see Christ be known and loved by all people, with the Church unified and sanctified, and sinners converted. We long for Jesus to return at last in all his glory.

---

6. Augustine, *Homily 4 on the First Epistle of John*, trans. H. Browne, in *Nicene and Post-Nicene Fathers*, first series, vol. 7, ed. Philip Schaff (Buffalo, NY: Christian Literature, 1888), rev. and ed. for New Advent by Kevin Knight, https://www.newadvent.org/fathers/170204.htm, no. 6.

Spiritual exercise

We can use small notebooks to write down passages of Scripture that impact us deeply, that shoot through us like arrows; brief words and phrases that help us to rekindle our desire for God.

. . . .

. . . .

. . . .

. . . .

3

Determination

SR. ANNE OF JESUS

> What He wishes for is the resolution which makes Him Master of your free will, for He needs no strength of ours. Indeed, His Majesty prefers to manifest His power in feeble souls, where it has more scope for work, and where He can better bestow the graces He longs to give.[1]
>
> —St. Teresa of Ávila

For those with a basic Carmelite education, the word *determination* immediately reminds us of Teresa of Ávila, who is well known for insisting on its importance. But do not be mistaken. Teresa (also known as *La Madre*) does not mean that our spiritual

1. Teresa of Ávila, *Conceptions of the Love of God*, chap. 3, no. 5, in *Minor Works of St. Teresa: Conceptions of the Love of God, Exclamations, Maxims and Poems of Saint Teresa of Jesus, trans. Benedictines of Stanbrook, rev. Benedict Zimmerman, OCD (Thomas Baker, 1913), p. 150*, https://archive.org/details/minorworksofstte00tere.

life and its fruitfulness depends on some kind of hand-wringing voluntarism. It is quite the opposite, in fact. Her experience shows us that this leads to nothing but a dead end. However, she does remind us of a great need to invest our will—our capacity for love—in following Christ.

Indispensable determination

How do you get started?

> . . . As I say, it is most important—all-important, indeed—that they should begin well by making an earnest and most determined resolve not to halt until they reach their goal [union with God], whatever may come, whatever may happen to them, however hard they may have to labour, whoever may complain of them, whether they reach their goal or die on the road or have no heart to confront the trials which they meet, whether the very world dissolves before them.[2]

This point is clear and powerful, especially if we refer back to the original text of this passage. Teresa of Ávila speaks of "a great and very strong determination." But as is common for her, *La Madre* does not just encourage

---

2. Teresa of Ávila, *The Way of Perfection*, trans. and ed. E. Allison Peers (Image Books, 1964), chap. 21, par. 2, https://ccel.org/ccel/teresa/way/way.i.xxvii.html.

us in this way. Her arguments appeal to our intelligence, awakening our desires with the aim of setting our hearts ablaze, and therefore motivating us deeply.

Why is this determination so important in our journey toward the ultimate goal of our life here on earth, that is union with God? First, it's worth all the effort! The beauty of this goal justifies our commitment to it. Second, there will be many challenges to face, and so we must not let ourselves be stopped or slowed down along the way. Finally, there is much at stake when we persevere in our spiritual life:

> . . . If by the help of God the beginner strives to reach the summit of perfection, I do not believe he will ever go to Heaven alone but will always take many others with him.[3]

Insufficient determination

Teresa of Ávila always taught from her own experiences, and not without going through pain and suffering. She nevertheless learned that no matter how strong our own (good) will is, it is not enough. God cannot be defeated. Living a spiritual life is not about achieving personal victories and success. If you rely purely on your own strength, you will never achieve your goals.

---

3. Teresa of Ávila, *The Life of Teresa of Jesus,* trans. and ed. E. Allison Peers (Image Books, 1960), chap. 11, par. 4, https://www.carmelitemonks.org/Vocation/teresa_life.pdf.

To be fruitful in spirit, therefore, we must combine our determination with a profound humility. This means, first and foremost, expecting everything from God, while also demonstrating our patience and trust that we will receive it. It's all about doing our part, but also understanding and experiencing the reality that we are deeply unable to save and change others. Therefore, this determination that is expected of us takes the form of our consent to God, and our openness to God's work: "What He wishes for is the resolution which makes Him Master of your free will."[4] God doesn't expect us to be heroes or champions of saintly virtue, but he does expect us to allow him take his rightful place in our lives.

"We must have great confidence, for . . . with God's help, if we make continual efforts to do so, we shall attain, though perhaps not at once, to that which many saints have reached through His favour,"[5] says Teresa of Ávila. The union with God is a long process. The great news is that it will succeed! Since it relies on God, of course it will succeed. But the process requires patience, perseverance, and a constant deepening of our trust in the power of God's grace.

---

4. Teresa of Ávila, *Conceptions of the Love of God*, p. 150.
5. Teresa of Ávila, *Life*, chap. 13, par. 2.

The right casting

One of the key parts of our spiritual life is that our role is above all to position ourselves so that God can accomplish his work in us and also through us. This is something on which Teresa of Ávila (and Carmelite spirituality in general) places great emphasis. God therefore has the main role in our spiritual lives. But he cannot "play his role" if we do not let him. We can sometimes unknowingly rob him of this, relying too much on our own efforts and giving him little to no control over our lives. If we allow him to play his role, God will gradually reshape our hearts, so that we can learn to "let go," not by taking away our responsibilities, but by placing us in our rightful place as his subjects, and as active contributors to his work. "*For apart from me, you can do nothing*" (Jn 15:5). This is what Jesus tells us. He does not say this to belittle us, but to set us free! It is such a relief to experience God as the constant in our lives. What a great weight off our shoulders! But what is our role in all of this? To commit ourselves with our entire being, and to place as few obstacles as possible to him acting in us and through us. In this way, the Lord can find in us a heart that is open to him. This requires a strong determination to act, especially when committing to a life of prayer. We should not forget that a life of prayer not only means counting how many times we faithfully pray to God; it also means searching for understanding between our present lives and the future.

Have faith that you will succeed

"You will reach your goal." So ends the Rule of St. Benedict. And St. Teresa tells us: "If anyone finds himself thus determined, there is nothing for him to fear."[6] This is true, we will achieve our goals. We will succeed in that sense. But this is not success in the context of purely our own achievements. What an encouragement this is for each and every one of us.

Teresa of Ávila can give us further valuable insights to reassure our hearts that we are on the right path, should we need this reassurance. "Our Lord conducts souls different ways," she tells us.[7] So do not fear that you are going in the wrong direction. God will always adapt and adjust to our individual qualities and to our individual ways of doing things. We have nothing to fear from God. The most important thing is that today, no matter who we are or how we are doing in life, we

6. Teresa of Ávila, *Life*, chap. 11, par. 12.

7. Teresa of Ávila, *Book of the Foundations*, trans. John Dalton (London: T. Jones, 1853), p. 100, https://archive.org/details/TheBookOfTheFoundations.

must decisively choose to follow him. And if we lack the confidence and determination to do this, do not simply give up. Instead, ask for God's grace and entrust yourself to the intercession of the Virgin Mary and Teresa of Ávila. By doing this, we will all succeed; not just as individuals but together.

Spiritual exercise

I thank the Lord for placing the desire in my heart to follow him. I ask him to strengthen my determination and deepen my trust in the power of his grace.

I ask the Lord to show me how I should position myself in relation to him, how I should let him "play his role" in my life, and how I should carry out my role.

. . . .

. . . .

. . . .

. . . .

4

Apostolic Zeal

FR. JEAN-LUC DU ST. NOM DE MARIE

Let us preserve the delightful and comforting joy of evangelizing, even when it is in tears that we must sow. May it mean for us . . . an interior enthusiasm that nobody and nothing can quench. May it be the great joy of our consecrated lives.[1]

—Pope St. Paul VI

We sometimes hear religious zeal referred to pejoratively or ironically as a synonym for preaching. In the modern secular world, when people zealously broadcast the gospel, even to believers, it can seem like exaggeration or even fundamentalism.

And yet, according to St. Thomas Aquinas, apostolic

1. Paul VI, Apostolic Exhortation Evangelii nuntiandi (December 8, 1975), no. 80. www.vatican.va.

zeal is not just an addition to a life of faith. It has a special place among Christian virtues. There is indeed a positive form of zeal, which is given to us by God. Perhaps if we reflect on this, we can discern and reconcile our zeal as an eagerness to live out our faith and to communicate it to others. In the end, only we ourselves know how much zeal we have for the gospel.

Passion

First of all, the perfect example of zeal for God and his purposes can be found in Jesus Christ. During the story of the merchants who were driven out of the temple in the Gospel according to St. John (see Jn 2), it is written that the disciples remember the verse from the Word: *"For zeal for thy house has consumed me"* (Ps 69:9). Jesus was consumed by his love for the Father. He was completely devoted to his mission. He did not fear hardship. He did not turn away from his calling, even until his death. His sole purpose on earth was to fulfill his Father's will. So, having a zeal for God means giving your whole life and heart to him as a living sacrifice, holding back nothing for yourself and your personal goals.

The prophet Elijah is filled with a sort of jealous zeal for the Lord (see 1 Kgs 19:10). In Hebrew, this jealousy comes in the form of a motivation to be closer to God. Zeal is therefore primarily a passion for God, a desire that pushes us to experience his love and transforms us into authentic witnesses who want to make it known to the world and to share it with others in the context of our personal calling. Zeal is also expressed in action: "*Never flag in zeal, be aglow with the Spirit, serve the Lord*" (Rom 12:11). Indeed, zeal is the fire that burns within us and pushes us to do things that we would never have dared to do before, much like the apostles at Pentecost.

Necessity

Pope Francis stated in his cycle of catechesis on evangelization that "When Christian life loses sight of the horizon of evangelization, the horizon of proclamation, it grows sick" and that "Without apostolic zeal, faith withers."[2]

From the Pauline perspective, zeal is just one part of the armor that Christians must wear for spiritual combat: "*Stand, therefore, . . . having shod your feet with the equipment of the gospel of peace*" (Eph 6:14–15). Zeal, translated here from the Greek *etoimasia*, consists not only of the attitude of someone who is alert and ready to act, but also consists of having a firm and

2. Francis, General Audience (January 11, 2023). www.vatican.va.

stable foundation that allows us to move forward, no matter what the terrain and challenges might be.

We may love God, but if we have no zeal, we risk defeat at the hands of the enemy. In the same way that we can't ride or run without the correct shoes, we can't serve God until the end without apostolic zeal.

Keeping the fire burning

When our apostolic zeal begins to fade, we should first question our faith in Christ and let his truth take root within us: Jesus is God's eternal answer to mankind's struggles. Let us be inspired by the passion of the holy preachers and evangelizers who committed their lives to the apostolate. Let us foster attitudes that open us up to the action of the Holy Spirit. In fact, as the Second Vatican Council said in its decree on the missionary activity of the Church,

> The Holy Spirit, who calls all men to Christ by the seeds of the Lord and by the preaching of the Gospel, stirs up in their hearts a submission to the faith. In the womb of the baptismal font, He begets to a new life those who believe in Christ.[3]

---

3. Second Vatican Council, Decree on the Mission Activity of the Church *Ad gentes divinitus*, (December 7, 1965), no. 15. www.vatican.va.

The Spirit urges each person to proclaim the gospel and understand the Word in the depths of their consciousness.

Criteria for good apostolic zeal

Jean-François Callens, nicknamed Doudou, was a married layman from the Community of the Beatitudes who died in 2014. He was a zealous preacher who explained some characteristics of the zeal that comes from God:

- Such zeal comes from God's will, not from one's own will and desires.

- Such zeal is selfless. It comes from our selfless readiness to do God's will.

- Such zeal stems from a love for God. It is forgetting about yourself and your own desires for the joy of God, the one we serve.

- Such zeal means making God's will your home. It means abandoning yourself, placing yourself into God's hands, and trusting him.

Conclusion

In summation, we must remember that it is in our spiritual life where we must be the most zealous. This is because everything we do for the kingdom of God must be with the aim of bearing fruit in our relationship with the Holy Spirit.

Apostolic zeal has its roots in self-sacrifice; it thrives in fraternal charity. It also gives spirit and energy to missionary life. Yet, everything must still be for the glory of God. It is passion manifesting as dedication, concern, service, and commitment. The ultimate goal of apostolic zeal is the salvation of souls. It therefore responds to Christ's desire to set the world ablaze with the fire of his love.

Apostolic zeal allows us to move forward without injury, like a soldier equipped for battle, whatever the difficulties of the terrain. The apostles braved all opposition and threats and were victorious (see Acts 4:20).

We need to have zeal because it not only allows us to follow Christ, but also allows us to engage in the battle that is proclaiming the gospel. Let us pray that we may have this zeal, as it strengthens us in our witness and allows our intention to serve the Lord to continue until the end. Let us ask for the Spirit of strength, determination, passion, and enthusiasm to empower us to be zealous witnesses to God and to inspire others to want to know Christ.

Spiritual exercise

Do I feel like I have hope for our world?

. . . .

. . . .

. . . .

. . . .

Where is my greatest treasure? What are my heart's thoughts and worries? Where are Christ and the gospel in my personal list of priorities?

. . . .

. . . .

. . . .

. . . .

The Virgin Mary often thought of others, not herself. This gave her a dynamic and enthusiastic attitude toward life. How do I react to the needs of people I see around me? Do I take an interest in others and make myself available?

. . . .

. . . .

. . . .

. . . .

5

Knowing God and Knowing Yourself

JOUMANA KHALIL

[You will] know the love of Christ which surpasses knowledge, that you may be filled with all the fulness of God.

—EPHESIANS 3:19

To know, in the biblical sense, is to enter into a personal relationship, to "understand" in the sense of knowledge "surrounding" you, to love, to unite. The Bible is full of the knowledge of God, because God wants to give us that intimacy of love that understands who we are, frees us, and allows us to become our true selves. Prayer is how we can grow in this knowledge. Is it not some profound dialogue between the soul and God that brings with it an intimacy that can unify our wills? But if prayer allows me to journey toward my own heart, it is above all because I am known, understood, loved, and saved.

God knows me

"Nathaniel said to him, 'How do you know me?' Jesus answered him, 'Before Philip called you, when you were under the fig tree, I saw you'" (Jn 1:48). *"Before I formed you in the womb I knew you, and before you were born I consecrated you; I appointed you a prophet to the nations"* (Jer 1:5). Prayer places me before the Living God, who is my Creator and my Savior. He has known me since before I was conceived, he has accompanied me on all my paths, he knows my heart better than anyone else, and he has always done so. Psalm 139 says this from beginning to end.

This knowledge is found in the presence and closeness of God, who is "more intimate to me than I am to myself."[1] In the words of St. Augustine: He knows me, and he wishes to reveal himself to me.

He invites me to know him in the Holy Spirit

"And this is eternal life, that they know thee the only true God, and Jesus Christ whom thou hast sent" (Jn 17:3).

The story of Adam and Eve shows us that the root of sin lies in the fear of God, which leads to distrust. This distrust can come from false images that occupy our minds, our subconscious, or our wounded hearts.

---

1. Augustine, *Confessions*, bk. 3, chap. 6, as paraphrased by Benedict XVI, General Audience (November 14, 2012). www.vatican.va.

But Jesus wants to give us access to the fruit that cures us of this: that is, the true knowledge of the Father who is "nothing but love and mercy," and a relationship with Jesus who gives us free access to eternal life.

"*The king has brought me into his chambers*" (Song 1:4), declares the beloved of the Song of Songs, aware that she is called to union with her spouse. These "chambers" remind us of the "inner castle" in its innermost chamber, the "enclosure" where God reveals himself to the soul and enables it to know him through the grace of the Holy Spirit. When I regularly and faithfully take the time to be silent and to listen, I experience a deeper knowledge of God through an inner light, an inspiration, or words from the Bible that shine a new light on me. "*A God merciful and gracious*" (Ps 86:15); "*God is love*" (1 Jn 4:16); "*I am the way, and the truth, and the life*" (Jn 14:6); "*the bridegroom*" (Mt 9:15; Mt 25:6; Jn 3:29); "*the Counselor*" (Jn 15:26, speaking of the Holy Spirit); and so on. Thus grows a spiritual knowledge that the contemplative grasps in a divine light: "This science of love, which elevates, enlightens, and enkindles, does not come by way of the understanding; a simple light, general and spiritual, it proceeds from God into the depths of the soul."[2]

2. Marie-Eugène de l'Enfant-Jésus, OCD, *I Want to See God: A Practical Synthesis of Carmelite Spirituality*, trans. M. Verda Clare, CSC (Fides, 1953), p. 499, https://archive.org/details/iwanttoseegodpra0000pmar.

Depending on how far one's thoughts are developed, the soul will come to know God to differing extents, from "faith being a knowledge of revealed truth" to a "transforming union" (this phrase comes from Teresa of Ávila, as related by Fr. Marie-Eugène de l'Enfant-Jésus).[3]

On the other hand, faithfully praying to God will sharpen your "spiritual senses"; these senses were spoken of by the Fathers of the Church. They are the sight, hearing, touch, smell, and taste of God. New spiritual dimensions are opened in man through prayer, and through your spirit, you are able to see God who is "with us," to hear him in his deepest heart and in his Word, to touch his presence, to smell his sweet fragrance and taste his goodness: "*O taste and see that the Lord is good!*" (Ps 34:8).

Through prayer, we acquire a form of spiritual light that leads to a greater knowledge of the self over time.

He invites me to know myself in him

"*Before I was aware, my fancy set me in a chariot beside my prince,*" sings the bride in the Song of Songs (6:12). This encounter with love will reveal to her who she truly is, as she discovers herself through the eyes of the Beloved. In this way, a knowledge of God goes hand

3. Marie-Eugène de l'Enfant-Jésus, *I Want to See God*, p. 28.

in hand with knowledge of the self. This is because a relationship with God reveals man to himself, and, as with any relationship involving trust, it breaks down our inner resistance: To be in God's presence is to be in the light of both love and truth, for this is where *"love and faithfulness will meet"* (Ps 85:10).

When my time of prayer becomes a silent encounter, I listen and welcome the Lord who watches over my happiness. He reveals to me the treasures that lay within me, the hidden beauty that makes me unique, my spiritual riches, the weaknesses I have, and the inadequacies I need to work on. In essence, God shows us our inner garden; the weeds we need to pull up from the root, the heavy stones we need to remove, and the dry branches we need to prune. Essentially, a life of prayer opens our eyes to the beauty that lies within us, as well as showing us everything that prevents our spiritual growth and a union with God: our sins, our attachments, our harmful tendencies, and so on.

By taking the time and paying faithful attention to God's constant presence within you, if you recognize your own strengths and weaknesses, you will become more vigilant, more aware of the inner workings of your heart, and more discerning of the voices inside; as a result, you will be able to recognize any jealous or judgmental thoughts as soon as they arise, and you can then replace them with a word of blessing instead. Furthermore, if any self-deprecating or self-critical thoughts appear, you will be able to look inwards toward yourself and find the humor in them. "Knowledge of oneself in the light of God will assure to the spiritual life [of the soul] its equilibrium, will make it human at the same time as sublime, practical as well as very elevated."[4] God loves to reveal himself to us, and he does this because he calls us his "friends." He reveals himself to us and he reveals us to ourselves.

Let us draw closer to this movement of love, where the focus is on being humble.

Spiritual exercise

I consider what God has revealed to me about himself, through his attributes. I reflect on this. I take the time to inwardly savor this "divine unveiling," and I ask him to reveal more of himself.

. . . .

. . . .

. . . .

. . . .

4. Marie-Eugène de l'Enfant-Jésus, *I Want to See God*, p. 35.

6

Treasure and Spiritual Poverty

FR. JACQUES PHILIPPE

The only good is to love God with all one's heart and to be here below poor in spirit.[1]

—St. Thérèse of Lisieux

Blessed are the poor

This is the first Beatitude from Matthew's Gospel, which serves as an introduction and encompasses all others: "*Blessed are the poor in spirit*" (Mt 5:3). This Beatitude holds a magnificent promise: that we can inherit of the kingdom of heaven, and personify the endless riches

1. Thérèse of Lisieux, Autobiographical Manuscripts, Manuscript A, p. 32, English transcript at Les Archives du Carmel de Lisieux, https://archives.carmeldelisieux.fr/en/archive/manuscrit-a/.

of a life with God. Essentially, this is the ultimate goal of a life with its basis in prayer. Spiritual poverty is therefore deeply connected with a life of prayer.

It is true that God can only fully communicate with those who are poor in heart; a heart that is free from human burdens. If my heart is burdened with emotional attachments and I search for security in other people, how can there be any room for God? To build a genuine life of prayer, we must labor to detach and strip ourselves of all that is not God, for God's sake.[2] We must learn to only rely on God, seeking no support outside of his infinite mercy and no security outside of his love.

Perseverance in prayer often means embracing poverty. This is the paradox of prayer: It offers immense riches, sometimes bringing us closer to heaven and filling our hearts in such a way that nothing else in this world can provide. Yet, at other times, it only brings a profound emptiness. The path to God's glory is one of poverty and humility. Reaching the mountaintop often requires enduring pain along the way.

Why is this? The first reason is that prayer is not some technique or process that guarantees success. It is not something that can be mastered, like a skill.

---

2. See John of the Cross, *The Ascent of Mount Carmel,* in *Collected Works,* bk. 2, chap. 5, p. 122.

Instead, prayer is a journey. It is an adventure during which we are entirely dependent on God. Sometimes, he may leave us to our struggles, and at other times, he may console us and fulfill us without us having done anything to deserve it. We can't manipulate or control God. Whatever God gives of himself is always free and unearned. It is a gift. Although he responds to those who seek him out, his response is never a direct result of our efforts, nor is it something we can predict.

The second reason is that perseverance in prayer draws us closer to God's light. This light can be gentle and comforting, but it can also be piercing and humbling. It is like a ray of sunlight illuminating a darkened room and exposing hidden dirt. God's divine light reveals our sins, our wounds, our hidden pride, and everything else within us that goes against the absolute purity of his love and the truth of the gospel.

Time spent in prayer is not always a time filled with joy and a sense of closeness with God. Sometimes there are moments of struggle and darkness. Sometimes, prayer can expose the problems in our lives, our deep dissatisfactions, and even our total helplessness. Although this may wound our sense of pride, it is necessary as it leads to our spiritual renewal. Healing can't happen if we are unaware of our illness. Therefore, we must confront the truth about ourselves if we want to be set free. Experiencing this sense of spiritual poverty, no matter how painful, strips away our grandiosity and our self-importance. It compels us to cry out to God for mercy. This is immensely valuable, as it teaches us to place our hope and trust in him rather than in ourselves. It also builds a deeper sense of compassion for others. How can I judge anyone else when I am so deeply aware of my own failings?

In this journey of spiritual life, particularly in prayer, God gradually takes away any possibility of relying on anything other than him. John Vianney, the Curé of Ars, once said: "God . . . has shown me this great mercy, that he has given me nothing on which I could rely, neither talent, nor wisdom, nor knowledge, nor strength, nor virtue."[3] Although it is true that our talents and our strengths should be used to serve God, it is a mistake to rely on them alone. We must place our reliance ultimately on God.

Faith, hope, charity, and spiritual poverty

A life of prayer has its basis in faith, hope, and love. However, each of these theological virtues carries with

---

3. John Vianney, *Thoughts of the Curé d'Ars*, comp. W. M. B. (Burns and Oates, 1930; repr. TAN Books, 1984), p. 46, https://archive.org/details/thoughts-cure-ars.

it an element of spiritual poverty. Faith requires us to believe without seeing, feeling, or fully understanding. Hope asks us to wait and trust in confidence that we will get what we long for, even if this is not yet ours. As St. Paul said, "*For in this hope we were saved. Now hope that is seen is not hope. For who hopes for what he sees?*" (Rom 8:24). To love is to embrace spiritual poverty: to live not for yourself, but for others. True love rejects any sense of ownership. To truly love someone is to welcome them and respect them without looking to control, manipulate, or own them.

Poverty and freedom

Before sending the apostles out on their mission, Jesus instructs them: "*You received without pay, give without pay*" (Mt 10:8). This Scripture is a cornerstone of the gospel and, in my opinion, is a perfect representation of spiritual poverty. Those who are truly poor can receive everything as a gift—not through entitlement, merit, claim, or status, but with pure simplicity, relying entirely on the generosity of the Giver.

The poor are able to give freely: They are not holding on to what they have received, nor using it to inflate their own ego, but instead they are offering it in service to others. Think of everything as a gift, instead of something that is owed to you. Never expect anything in return. Always see yourself as an unworthy servant who has simply done their duty. Do not look for recognition or reward for what has been achieved. This is true wisdom. If we receive only what we deserve, we would not be receiving much. But if we place our hope in God's limitless mercy, the rewards will be far greater!

This is why Thérèse of Lisieux says, "There is no joy comparable to that enjoyed by the truly poor in spirit."[4] In this context, her sense of joy comes from a deep sense of freedom, a detachment from all things. Those who are truly poor in spirit have nothing to defend or lose, because they have already surrendered everything to God. They expect all things from him. By losing themselves in God, they gain everything. What's more, if I am genuinely poor in spirit in both my apostolic work and my relationships, I will be able to offer myself to God completely. But if I am entirely self-sufficient, I will share only my opinions, my ideas, and my personal beliefs. Only with a heart without self-interest and pride can God's work shine through us with clarity and purity.

4. Thérèse of Lisieux, Autobiographical Manuscripts, Manuscript C, p. 16.

Spiritual exercise

In prayer, I can ask for God's grace to help me recognize how my weaknesses can in fact be blessings. How can the Lord transform them into opportunities for humility, joy, and simplicity? What benefits have these brought into my life today?

. . . .

. . . .

. . . .

. . . .

I take a moment to reflect on the words of Thérèse of Lisieux regarding spiritual poverty:

> . . . You have to agree to remain poor and without strength and that is the difficult thing because "The truly poor in spirit, where to find him? you have to look for it far away" said the psalmist . . . He does not say that you have to look for it among great souls, but "far away," that is to say in baseness, in nothingness. . . . Oh! so let's stay far away from everything that shines, love our littleness, love to feel nothing, then we will be poor in spirit and Jesus will come to get us, however far we are he will transform us into flames of love.[5]

---

5. Thérèse of Lisieux, Letter to Sr. Marie of the Sacred Heart, September 17, 1896, Thérèse's Correspondence, Les Archives du Carmel de Lisieux, https://archives.carmeldelisieux.fr/en/correspondance/lt-197-a-soeur-marie-du-sacre-coeur-17-septembre-1896/.

7

A Life in Reflection

SR. MARIE-BÉNÉDICTE JAULME

Man is created to praise, reverence, and serve God our Lord, and by this means to save his soul. And the other things on the face of the earth are created for man and that they may help him in prosecuting the end for which he is created.[1]

—Ignatius of Loyola

Why should you reflect upon your life?

God is continually working in our lives. Reflecting on our experiences allows us to recognize and appreciate how the Lord is actively shaping and guiding us through life.

1. Ignatius of Loyola, *The Spiritual Exercises*, trans. Elder Mullan, SJ (Kenedy, 1914), "Principle and Foundation," p. 14, https://www.ccel.org/ccel/ignatius/exercises.xii.i.html.

In everyday life, God reveals himself through events, encounters, and prayer. Reflecting on our lives is valuable for recognizing how God has worked within us. It involves recognizing and remembering the blessings that he has given us and understanding how he guides us and reveals himself in ways that are unique and personal to us. This helps us to better understand his will, to discern his calling for us, and to make choices that line up with a life lived with God. Although major life events can lead us to deeply reconsider our lives, it is vital to first build the habit of reflecting like this on a smaller scale–day by day.

How can I do this?

This reflecting can be achieved through a brief prayer every day. This prayer can last ten to fifteen minutes, either during the day or at night, with the aim of reflecting on how God's presence has been a part of my day and how I responded to him. For this to be effective, it must be done every day. Doing this consistently helps in two ways: first, daily prayer makes it a habit and therefore it is easier to establish this as a routine; second, without regularly reflecting on my day, it is difficult to clearly remember the events of the day.

Before starting my review of the day, I take a moment to remember God's purpose for my life. As St. Ignatius said, the ultimate goal of the Christian life is that the Lord

> Take . . . and receive all my liberty, my memory, my intellect, and all my will—all that I have and possess. Thou gavest it to me: to Thee, Lord, I return it! All is Thine, dispose of it according to all Thy will. Give me Thy love and grace, for this is enough for me.[2]

It is a question of confronting my true identity and my purpose as children of God, and aligning myself with the deepest desires of my hearts. The first step is gratitude. It is vital that I recognize that God is present and working in my life, and to give thanks for it.

Therefore I am firmly rooted in my primary purpose: giving thanks.

I begin my daily prayer by reflecting on what happened today, allowing the memories of the day to resurface in my mind. I focus on recognizing what God has blessed me with today—the moments that strengthened me, energized me, and deepened my relationship with him, with others, and with myself. In the Ignatian tradition, this is referred to as the "good spirit" emerging from the kingdom of God and

---

2. Ignatius of Loyola, *Spiritual Exercises*, p. 69.

rising within me. If I pay close attention, one, two, or even three key moments in my day may stand out. In this way, I can clearly recognize several signs of God's presence in my life.

This first step brings up memories in the heart—the spiritual memory. It comes from the movement of the heart. It is not an intellectual exercise. When this step is complete, I rejoice before the Lord, giving thanks for all he has given me and for the gift of my relationship with him.

Once the first step is complete, I can move on to the second: reconciliation. I reflect on my day again, but this time it is on the good things that I rejected—what I could have received, what I could have given to others and to myself, and what others could have given me. In essence, we reconcile with what we might call the "evil spirit." Again, two or three specific things will likely come to mind. At this point, I will express my regret and grieve before the Lord, who is infinitely good and merciful. Despite my sins, the Lord calls to me, trusts me, and sets me on the correct path again. He waits for me to continue the journey. And in this, I will find joy.

This stage of reconciliation involves three key parts: reclaiming what has been denied to me, mourning and regretting the loss, and rejoicing in the goodness of the Lord, who continues to call out to me in spite of this. By doing this, I move past the bitterness of sin, the sorrow I feel, and the plea for forgiveness. I move forward into the joy of being renewed.

Finally, I consider the following day. Where will the Lord ask me to take action? Will this be at work? In my relationships? Or perhaps I will need to make a difficult decision? I entrust the upcoming day to him through a brief prayer of trust, and I embrace the new path to which he is calling me. I know that God is waiting for me on this path, and I am confident that he will walk beside me.

The benefits of this exercise

The first benefit of this daily reflection is that we learn how to listen to God and the Holy Spirit deeply, and how to discern the good spirits from the bad; in essence, we are developing the ability to recognize what comes from God and what does not. I will gradually become more attuned to noticing God at work in my day, my week, and even over the past month. Building this habit into my day helps me to better understand and interpret my experiences with the Lord.

I can also make brief notes on what I discover, which is an invaluable tool for both the spiritual review and the stage of reconciliation.

Over time, I will develop a deeper awareness of my inner desires, experiences, and daily accomplishments. This heightened awareness will help me to recognize whether I am aligning with the Holy Spirit or withdrawing into myself. Ultimately, this exercise sharpens our spiritual senses, developing the inner mindfulness that the Desert Fathers emphasized in their tradition of discernment. This is a powerful tool in our spiritual growth.

Conclusion

Reflecting on our day is a spiritual exercise that we can all take part in. We simply need to make the decision to implement it and to have the perseverance to maintain it daily. This allows us to reap the benefits that the Lord wants us to have. This daily practice invites us to review our lives, so we can recognize God's presence and his work within them.

Once this daily spiritual exercise has been established, it becomes easier to reflect on our life over a longer period of time. Making regular notes on this becomes a valuable resource, helping us to remember God's presence and his actions throughout the months and years, as well as our struggles and temptations.

By doing this, we can recognize the common thread in our life. It helps us to recognize how God is guiding us in the present moment, and to identify the specific challenges that we are currently facing.

Spiritual exercise

I am making it a habit to reflect on my day.

1. I make the Sign of the Cross/I center myself/I gather my thoughts.
2. I call upon the Holy Spirit.
3. I align myself with my life's purpose: "May everything I desire, everything I do, and everything I achieve be solely directed toward the service and worship of God."
4. I give thanks, in the following ways:
   - I reflect on the key moments of the day, recognizing them as signs of God's presence and work in my life.
   - I rejoice in the presence of the Lord, the source of all life.
5. I allow myself to be reconciled, in the following ways:
   - I allow the moments in my day when I rejected God to resurface in my memory.
   - I am truly sorry for this, and I deeply regret it before the Lord.
   - Despite my sins, the Lord calls out to me, trusts me, and relies on me–and for this, I rejoice.

6. I will follow the Lord.
7. I end with a prayer that I enjoy, followed by making the Sign of the Cross.

. . . .

. . . .

. . . .

. . . .

8

Why Be Accompanied?

SR. THERESIA SCHUSCHNIGG

To gain access to his fully developed humanity, something of this place of God within will need to manifest itself to human consciousness, to be progressively integrated with it.[1]

—André Louf

The spiritual life: a journey in progress

Every Christian, no matter if they are consciously aware of it or not, is called to live both by the Spirit and in the Spirit, and to grow over time into a profound life of union with God. When it comes to a *life* of union with God that is a spiritual life, it is far from a trivial thing. This *life* is fundamentally rooted in our experiences

1. André Louf, *Grace Can Do More: Spiritual Accompaniment and Spiritual Growth*, trans. Susan Van Winkle (Cistercian 2002), p. 37, https://archive.org/details/gracecandomoresp0000louf.

with God; these are experiences that nurture our relationship with him, with ourselves, and with the world around us. It is a question of our encounters, rather than simply our thoughts. This spiritual journey is complex, is filled with a shared understanding and connection, and enables the dynamic process of growth.

This of course raises several questions. How can we recognize whether an experience is truly from God and not simply a product of our imagination or desires? Is this genuinely God at work, or is it just my own psyche? Am I deceiving myself? Such doubts inevitably arise when we only talk about God, instead of truly speaking with him. This is exactly the point in *life* where the need for guidance is crucial. Everyone who is living a spiritual life and seeks to experience God needs some spiritual direction—whether you are a seasoned veteran who has walked this path for many years, or new to this path and only just beginning to take your first steps.

The purpose of spiritual guidance

What is the purpose of receiving guidance from others? Ultimately, it is to deepen our experience of God. Although this may sound straightforward, it is often challenging in practice. Speaking with others about our encounters with God is not easy—it touches the core of our innermost being, and this can naturally evoke some resistance. As a result, we may be tempted to change the subject to other topics: our own worries, doubts, hopes, plans, questions, or ideas. We might turn to a friend or someone in our community for some empathetic listening, encouragement, comfort, solutions to our problems, or validation of our choices—or even someone to make decisions for us. However, "The rock [that we seek] is not any other human being, but the mystery we call God, as that mystery is experienced in each person's own heart and mind and spirit."[2]

Above all, it is the other person's responsibility to guide the conversation and avoid taking on a role that is not theirs to take. However, as we are the ones being supported, we also have a significant level of responsibility. When we acknowledge our need for spiritual guidance, we can take steps to prepare and approach it with greater awareness and intentionality.

When we say that the focus of guidance is to better live a spiritual life, it clearly goes beyond simply our moments of prayer. Everyone is called to strive for continuous prayer—that is, to seek out God in all

---

2. William A. Barry and William J. Connolly, *The Practice of Spiritual Direction*, (Seabury Press, 1982) chap. 2, p. 16.

aspects of our lives. Prayer becomes continuous when we consistently direct our attention toward God, not only during the times that we dedicate to prayer but also in our work, relationships, free time, and every other part of our daily lives. Therefore, anything that happens in our daily life can be shared during a spiritual conversation. However, we will not focus on what happened or our personal feelings and reactions. Instead, we will focus on

> that dimension of any experience that evokes the presence of the mysterious Other whom we call God. Moreover, this experience is viewed, not as an isolated event, but as an expression of the ongoing personal relationship God has established with each one of us.[3]

If we truly believe in a God who is both living and present, it is logical to conclude that this same God is alive and active in every moment of our daily lives. The purpose of spiritual guidance is to become consciously aware of God's presence in us and in our lives. Only when we fully realize this awareness, can we then truly answer God's call.

---

3. Barry and Connolly, *Practice of Spiritual Direction*, chap. 1, p. 8.

Discerning spirits

The main purpose of spiritual guidance is to help us discern what comes from our minds and what comes from our hearts. Through this guidance, we can closely examine our experiences with God and together we can seek to understand his true nature. We can then work to deepen our understanding and learn to recognize our response to the calls from God that may arise within us. As it is said,

> . . . Yet life is not without the threat of death, the non-accomplishment of promise. A life can become sickly, paralyzed, it can suffocate and finally be extinguished. Nothing remains immutable because life does not stand still.[4]

The main purpose of following this path is to allow God to work directly within us, his creation, and to foster an environment in which he can carry out his essential work within us. The role of the guide is to help us focus solely on God, guiding us toward him and attuning us to his voice without relying on a go-between.

Why do we invite you to join us?

– We believe in a God who is profoundly real and who is "present, interested, involved, available for real interaction: and more than that–initiating, acting,

4. Louf, *Grace Can Do More*, p. 33.

relating, desiring and responding."[5] We desire to live out our faith authentically.

– We need a brother or sister in faith to help us examine our experiences with the living God more deeply. This support from others allows us to gradually build trust in the knowledge we can have of him and to have a face-to-face encounter with the God who has become real in our lives.

– We must always remain focused on the central question of human existence: Who is God to me, and who am I to him?

How should I prepare for a spiritual interview?

1. Reflect on your most recent spiritual talk about God: What insights or realizations came up during my last conversation about God and myself? How have these thoughts or experiences developed since then?
2. Reflect on the weeks that have passed since your last spiritual talk: What were the key events that had an impact on me? How have they influenced me? What emotions did I feel?

---

5. Robert R. Marsh, "Teaching Spiritual Direction as If God Were Real," *The Way* 53, no. 4 (2014), p. 57, https://www.theway.org.uk/back/534Marsh.pdf.

3. Prayer:
   - I stand in God's presence and reflect on how he has been present at various times of my life. What message is he conveying to me, and how is he guiding me or working in my life?
   - I tune into my soul: What do I feel? How do I react inwardly? What are my desires? How would I like to respond?

Spiritual exercise

I take the time to reflect on my journey of spiritual guidance, including its blessings and challenges, and I offer it to the Lord.

. . . .

. . . .

. . . .

. . . .

9

Sanctifying Your Space

ODILE HAUMONTÉ

The Lord is my shepherd, I shall not want; he makes me lie down in green pastures. He leads me beside still waters; he restores my soul. He leads me in paths of righteousness for his name's sake. Even though I walk through the valley of the shadow of death, I fear no evil; for thou art with me. . . . Surely goodness and mercy shall follow me all the days of my life; and I shall dwell in the house of the Lord for ever.

—PSALM 23:1-4, 6

In the beginning . . .

In the beginning, on the third day of Creation,

> And God said, "Let the waters under the heavens be gathered together into one place, and let the dry land appear." And it was so. God called the

> dry land Earth, and the waters that were gathered together he called Seas. And God saw that it was good. (Gn 1:9–10)

This earth, therefore, was given to us to fill. But it came only after the creation of light on the first day, and after heaven on the second. This symbolic account of our origins reminds us that our earthly existence is temporary. It is granted to us for a purpose: to prepare the way and to fulfill our mission, as we are ultimately called to dwell in the heart of the Lord and to live in his eternal light.

A holy ground

God appeared to Abraham and said: "*Now the Lord said to Abram, 'Go from your country and your kindred and your father's house to the land that I will show you'*" (Gn 12:1). To those who obey and follow him, God promises a holy place where they can encounter him. Many generations later, while Moses was tending to his father-in-law's sheep, he led them to graze at the base of Mount Horeb. There he saw a bush that was burning but was not consumed by the flames. Curious, Moses went out of his way to investigate, and God called out to him from within the bush. As Moses approached, the Lord spoke and gave him a command: "*Then he said, 'Do not come near; put off your shoes from your feet, for the place on which you are standing is holy ground. . . . I know their sufferings'"* (Ex 3:5–7). God reveals himself to his people, when they have lost all hope, and promises to lead them out of slavery into freedom, from a foreign land to their rightful inheritance: "*And I will bring you into the land which I swore to give to Abraham, to Isaac, and to Jacob*" (Ex 6:8). After many trials and tribulations, the people would finally inherit the Promised Land—a place of joy and rest. However, this land was not yet the sacred site where they could fully encounter God. In Jerusalem, the holy city, an even more sacred place was to be built: the temple. Solomon built the temple using fine wood, adorned it with gold and jewels, and offered prayers to dedicate it: "*that thy eyes may be open day and night toward this house, the place where thou hast promised to set thy name, that thou mayest hearken to the prayer which thy servant offers toward this place*" (2 Chr 6:20). However, despite the blessing upon it, the temple was destroyed. People were in fact not looking for a specific place, a "gateway" of communication with God, but for a real encounter with him, a face-to-face meeting. From orphaned humanity rises the cry we hear every year in the liturgy at the beginning of Advent: "*O that thou wouldst rend the heavens and come down*" (Is 64:1). We can't rise up to meet you, Lord . . . so Lord, come down to us!

The true worshippers

In response to our deep longing for this encounter, God opened the heavens and chose to live among us. However, he was not born in the grandeur of Herod's palace. Instead, Jesus was born in a humble stable because there was no room for the Holy Family in the homes of Bethlehem. He sanctified many places with his presence: the temple, the synagogue in Capernaum, the shores of Lake Tiberias, the wedding hall in Cana, and many more. Yet, he never made any of these places his permanent residence–not even the temple, whose destruction he foretold. He often retreated to deserted places to pray and he even taught us to pray in private, discretely in our bedrooms. When the Samaritan woman asked the proper place for worship, saying, "*You say that in Jerusalem is the place where men ought to worship,*" Jesus responded that from that point forward, the physical location would no longer be important. "*But the hour is coming, and now is, when the true worshipers will worship the Father in spirit and truth, for such the Father seeks to worship him*" (Jn 4:20–23). Jesus announces a new temple, one that is "*not made with hands*" (Mk 14:58), and St. John adds: "*But he spoke of the temple of his body*" (Jn 2:21).

The inner fortress

In Judaism, the *Minyan* rule states that when ten adult men come together, they form a quorum and are permitted to recite the prayers of the liturgy or worship services. For us Christians, Jesus said: "*For where two or three are gathered in my name, there am I in the midst of them*" (Mt 18:20).

Carmelite prayer invites us to discover within ourselves the sacred space of true worshippers. Teresa of Ávila wrote to her Carmelite sisters,

> Those who are able to shut themselves up in this way within this little Heaven of the soul, wherein dwells the Maker of Heaven and earth, . . . may be sure that they are walking on an excellent road.[1]

St. John of the Cross echoed this, saying,

> God, then, is hidden in the soul, and there the good contemplative must seek Him with love, exclaiming: "Where have You hidden . . . ?" Oh, then, soul . . . you yourself are His dwelling and His secret chamber and hiding place.[2]

This is why we can pray anywhere—whether in the quiet of our room or in the heart of St. Peter's Square,

---

1. Teresa of Ávila, *The Way of Perfection*, chap. 28, par. 6
2 John of the Cross, *Spiritual Canticle*, in *Collected Works*, p. 418.

in the stillness of the desert or the chaos of the subway, kneeling before the tabernacle or stuck in traffic.

The Real Presence and signs

"He is here!" exclaimed the saintly Curé of Ars as he placed the consecrated Host in the tabernacle. God, who fills the universe, is truly present; even in a small piece of bread which is transformed into his Body. Although he calls upon us to live by faith and through faith, God understands our need for clear signs so that our devotion to him can be sustained. This is what we mean by gestures that help us to manifest the invisible realities in our lives and in our surroundings: the beauty of our churches, the Calvaries along our roadsides, the crosses in our homes, and the lovingly adorned corners dedicated to prayer.

"He is here," in our churches, homes, and hearts until the very end, having walked the human path with his feet. As we await the heavenly Jerusalem, let us cultivate the soul of a pilgrim: let us love this land we travel through, and do everything we can to make it more beautiful and peaceful, knowing that we are only passing through.

Spiritual exercise

Do I feel like a "citizen of heaven," knowing that's where I will spend eternity?

. . . .

. . . .

. . . .

. . . .

Do I feel free inside to "leave my country" like Abraham did, and go to the place that God will reveal to me?

. . . .

. . . .

. . . .

. . . .

Am I willing to step out of my comfort zone and break free from my routines to embrace the courage needed for new encounters?

. . . .

. . . .

. . . .

. . . .

I can pray with St. Thérèse to discover within myself that sacred place where God wishes to meet me:

> Your Face is my only homeland.
> It's my Kingdom of love.
> It's my cheerful meadow.[3]

---

3. Thérèse of Lisieux, "Canticle to the Holy Face," in *The Poetry of Saint Thérèse of Lisieux*, trans. Donald Kinney, OCD (ICS, 2013), p. 33.

10

Sanctifying Your Time

ODILE HAUMONTÉ

I've just this fleeting day to form
This cluster of love, whose seeds are souls.
Ah! give me, Jesus, the fire of an Apostle
Just for today.[1]

—St. Thérèse of Lisieux

"*And there was evening and there was morning, one day*" (Gn 1:5). From the very beginning, God—who exists beyond time—created time itself. Creation closely follows the rhythm of life: our heart beats, we breathe in and out—all of these processes create in us a biological rhythm. Plants, animals, and humans—

1. Thérèse of Lisieux, "My Song for Today," Poems—PN 05, Les Archives du Carmel de Lisieux, https://archives.carmeldelisieux.fr/en/archive/pn-5/.

every living being–is created "*according to its kind*"[2] and, we might say, according to its unique rhythm.

God places us in time: "*The years of our life are threescore and ten, or even by reason of strength fourscore*" (Ps 90:10) so that we may fill it with his grace and presence.

Dedicating one day to the Lord

Of all the Ten Commandments given by God to Moses, the first two focus on God himself, while the last seven look into relationships between people. At the center lies the third commandment, which emphasizes the importance of finding rest in God. This serves as a bridge between God and mankind:

> Observe the sabbath day, to keep it holy, as the Lord your God commanded you. Six days you shall labor, and do all your work; but the seventh day is a sabbath to the Lord your God; in it you shall not do any work. (Dt 5:12–15)

The Sabbath day invites us to reflect on and celebrate God's presence as he works in our lives. Sunday, the day of the Resurrection, is both the first day of the week and the eighth day, symbolizing the fulfillment of creation and the promise of the world to come. The name *Sunday* comes from the Latin terms *dies Domini* or *dies dominica*, meaning "the Lord's Day."

---

2. This phrase is used repeatedly in the following bible passages: Gn 1:11–25; Gn 6:20; Gn 7:14; Lv 11:14–29.

For three centuries, the first Judeo-Christians continued to observe both the Sabbath day and Sunday. Over time, however, Sunday—the day on which the Eucharist was celebrated—took precedence over the Sabbath day. "We move from the 'Sabbath' to the 'first day after the Sabbath,' from the seventh day to the first day: the *dies Domini* becomes the *dies Christi*!," St. John Paul II explains about the sanctification of Sunday.[3]

Sanctifying our Sundays

Whereas the Sabbath Day is to remember Creation, Sunday celebrates the new creation brought about by Jesus. "In effect, Sunday is the day above all other days which summons Christians to remember the salvation which was given to them in baptism and which has made them new in Christ."[4] Just as Jesus is "*Lord of the Sabbath*" (Mt 12:8), may he also be the honored guest of our Sundays. Let us embrace Sundays as a brief insight into the eternal joy we will feel when we will behold him in eternity.

> We need this encounter which brings us together, which gives us space for freedom, which lets us see beyond the bustle of everyday life to God's creative

3. John Paul II, Apostolic Letter on Keeping the Lord's Day Holy *Dies Domini* (May 31, 1998), no. 18. www.vatican.va.
4. John Paul II, *Dies Domini*, no. 25.

love, from which we come and towards which we are travelling.[5]

St. John Vianney, the Curé of Ars, understood very well that young people need moments of joy and celebration to lift their spirits after a week of hard work. He therefore provided this by organizing Christian festivals and processions on Sunday afternoons. "Sunday is the property of our good God," he would say. "What right have you to meddle with what does not belong to you?"[6]

Pray continuously

God gives us our time so that we can fill it with his presence through prayer and gratitude. "*Rejoice always, pray constantly . . . for this is the will of God in Christ Jesus for you*" (1 Thes 5:16–18). Praying continuously is a challenge for every Christian. How can we make time for prayer in our busy lives, where every activity feels like a race against the clock?

Of course, it can be difficult to find the time to stop and pray in a church or even in the quiet of our bedroom. However, we often have many "empty"

---

5. Benedict XVI, Homily, St. Stephen's Cathedral, Vienna (September 9, 2007). www.vatican.va.

6. Alfred Monnin, *The Spirit of the Curé of Ars*, trans. and ed. John Edward Bowden (London: Burns, Lambert, and Oates, 1865), p. 59.

moments throughout our day that we could fill with prayer instead of scrolling through our phones: during commutes, while ironing or cleaning, standing in line, exercising, walking, waiting for pasta to cook, or even while driving. These seemingly "lost" moments are actually opportunities for spiritual connection. As Thérèse of Lisieux once said of Our Lord, "I really believe that I have never been three minutes without thinking of the good Lord."[7]

Our daily bread

When we address God in the Lord's Prayer:

"Give us *this day* our *daily* bread." How often do we truly think about the words we speak? We rarely savor the moment or the place we find ourselves in. Instead, we think of times and places in the past and the future that do not fulfil us because no one is waiting for us there. The grace that is meant to fill our souls only exists in the present, but if we are not existing in the present moment, it withers like a flower without water, leaving us unhappy with both our day and ourselves. We must let go of our regrets about the past and our

7. Quoted in Geneviève of the Holy Face, *Advice and Memories from a Novice*, Les Archives du Carmel de Lisieux, https://archives.carmeldelisieux.fr/en/au-carmel-du-temps-de-therese/la-communaute/soeur-genevieve-de-la-sainte-face/conseils-et-souvenirs-dune-novice/.

fantasies about the future—thoughts like "When my children were little . . ." or "When my children are grown up . . . ," "When I live somewhere else . . .," or "When I achieve this goal or that goal." Instead, let us fully embrace this present day. Let us savor the beauty and goodness of this present moment, a moment that we'll never experience again: the here and now.

Each morning

Cardinal Léon Joseph Suenens embraced a spirituality of gratitude, saying, "I am an optimist because I believe the Holy Spirit is the Spirit of creation. To those who welcome him he gives each day fresh liberty and renewed joy and trust."[8] Every single morning! Day after day! The Lord provides us with the strength, joy, kindness, courage, and hope that we need. Day after day, he walks with us.

This allows us to start our day by offering to God the ever-renewed opportunity he graciously provides us.

Spiritual exercise

Am I avoiding the reality of the present by constantly jumping from one thing to another, never fully engaged in what I'm doing?

---

8. Léon Joseph Suenens, *A New Pentecost?*, trans. Francis Martin (Seabury Press, 1975), p. xiii.

. . . .

. . . .

. . . .

. . . .

Do I dwell on the past? Am I consumed with regret and remorse?

. . . .

. . . .

. . . .

. . . .

Am I worried about the future? Psychologists say that 95 percent of the fears we have about the future never actually come true.

. . . .

. . . .

. . . .

. . . .

Each day, I find comfort in reciting this reminder by Br. Roger of Taizé: "God is never, never at all, a tormentor of the human conscience. He buries our past in the heart of Christ and is going to take care of our future."[9]

---

9. Roger of Taizé, *God Is Love Alone* (Continuum, 2003), p. 32.

11

Why *Lectio Divina?*

SR. MARIE PIA ZURBACH

If a man loves me, he will keep my word, and my Father will love him, and we will come to him and make our home with him.

—JOHN 14:23

Introduction

Every believer has the privilege of hearing the Word of God during Mass. Is that not enough? So why do we practice *lectio divina*? What does it involve, and what does it offer us?

First, let us hear Benedict XVI's response to these questions:

> In this context, I would like in particular to recall and recommend the ancient tradition of *Lectio divina*: the diligent reading of Sacred Scripture accompanied by

> prayer brings about that intimate dialogue in which the person reading hears God who is speaking, and in praying, responds to him with trusting openness of heart (See *Dei Verbum*, no. 25). If it is effectively promoted, this practice will bring to the Church–I am convinced of it–a new spiritual springtime.[1]

Who would not want such a "springtime," both for themselves and for everyone around them?

A light

In *lectio divina*, we engage in a deep and prolonged communion with the one who calls himself "*the light of the world*" (Jn 8:12). By listening attentively, reflecting on the Word we receive, and praying through it, we grow to know God's heart more deeply, as God desires to reveal himself to us. Gradually, we acquire a greater understanding of both ourselves and the nature of the human heart.

The Word of God, embraced more deeply through *lectio*, will provide clarity to our thoughts and guide us in our daily actions. It will support us in making both small and significant choices in our lives and will help us to behave as "*children of light*" (Eph 5:8) The Word of God will become, more and more, "*a lamp to my feet*" (Ps 119:105).

---

1. Benedict XVI, Address to the International Congress for the 40th Anniversary of the Dogmatic Constitution *Dei Verbum* (September 16, 2005). www.vatican.va.

"*Living and active, sharper than any two-edged sword, piercing to the division of soul and spirit*" (Heb 4:12), it will help us discern within ourselves what is truly fitting for a disciple of Jesus and what is not.

Food for thought

The Word of God is often likened to a form of food for humanity, or an essential nourishment. Jesus, drawing upon words spoken to Israel in the wilderness, (see Dt 8:3), emphasizes this truth during his own time of testing in the desert: "*Man shall not live by bread alone, but by every word that proceeds from the mouth of God*" (Mt 4:4). Ancient writers often refer to "chewing" or "chewing over" the Word, and sometimes use the term "manducation" to describe this process. This practice involves repeating a verse, turning it over and over in our minds, therefore allowing it to sink deeply into our memory and our hearts. Through this, the Word enriches and transforms us.

St. Bernard emphasizes the "delight" of this practice: "To linger amid these truths is my delight; my heart is enlarged, my whole inward being is enriched, my very bones vibrate with praise."[2] This means taking the time to sit and meditate on the Word of God—long enough to savor it like a meal!

2. Bernard of Clairvaux, *On the Song of Songs I*, Sermon 16, no. 2, p. 115.

In *Lectio Divina*, the Word "descends" into our hearts and guides us toward prayer and a deeper encounter with God. It can also enrich our moments of adoration, especially when we are not naturally deep thinkers.

A renewal

The Word of God is inherently creative, as we can see in the Bible: "*For thou didst speak, and they were made. Thou didst send forth thy Spirit, and it formed them*" (Jdt 16:14). Jesus, the Word made flesh, calls Lazarus out of his tomb with a single, brief command. At this point, he had been dead for four days. One word from God, received with faith and full attention, is surely enough to restore and renew us completely.

But we know that because we hear and speak so many words, some are heard only once: "*Arise, shine; for your light has come*" (Is 60:1). Once is often not enough for the Word to truly have an impact on us and reveal the fullness of the "life" it holds within. We must slow our usual reading pace and embrace the words in our hearts as a small "seed" of life. It takes time—time to reflect, meditate, question, and allow the Word to transform into prayer. Only then can it deeply take root in our memory and eventually shape our actions. We must also make sure that thorns and brambles do not stop the Word from growing (see Mk 4:7) and prevent it from reaching full maturity.

If we dedicate time to the Word each day, we can see how the Word transforms us (sometimes gently, sometimes powerfully), revealing our true identity as sons and daughters of the Father.

Meditation, therefore, has the power to renew our hearts, as Matta El Meskeen so eloquently expresses:

> The perseverance of the heart in meditating on the Scriptures always results in a true infusion of life into the heart; for the Word of God, as defined by the Lord, is Spirit and Life . . . . Meditation on the Law of God keeps the heart alive, warmed by the fire of the divine Word; for meditation fundamentally encompasses the continuous deepening of the spirit of the Scriptures and the search for the truths hidden behind the commandment. This results in the constant renewal of a person's thoughts, refining their sensitivity to become more evangelical, and granting them a flexible and easy demeanor, positively open to all possibilities.[3]

As we move forward with *Lectio Divina*, even greater treasures await us:

> . . . For in the sacred books, the Father who is in heaven meets His children with great love and speaks with them; and the force and power in the word of God is so great

3. Matta El Meskeen, *L'expérience de Dieu dans la vie de prière* (Éd. Abbaye de Bellefontaine, 2019), pp. 50–51. All quotes from this book are our translation.

that it stands as the support and energy of the Church, the strength of faith for her sons, the food of the soul, the pure and everlasting source of spiritual life.[4]

Spiritual exercise

I will choose a psalm that is especially meaningful to me.

. . . .

. . . .

. . . .

. . . .

I choose one or two verses to memorize.

. . . .

. . . .

. . . .

. . . .

I then reflect on what the Lord wants to show me through these few words.

. . . .

. . . .

. . . .

. . . .

4. Second Vatican Council, Dogmatic Constitution on Divine Revelation *Dei verbum* (November 18, 1965), no. 21. www.vatican.va.

12

How Do We Engage in *Lectio Divina*?

SR. MARIE PIA ZURBACH

The meditation of the Scriptures is the first door of access to the wisdom of the Spirit and to all divine knowledge.[1]

—St. Isaac the Syrian

Introduction

Lectio divina is a slow reading of the Word of God, involving meditation and prayer, which is designed so that we can be deeply influenced and transformed by it. The purpose of *lectio divina* is to guide us from the written text to a personal encounter with the living God. Sometimes, when we first read a biblical

1. St. Isaac the Syrian, *Fonds arabe*, I, 5, 87; cited in Matta El Meskeen, *L'expérience de Dieu*, no. 26, p. 58.

passage, we may feel captivated by a word or phrase that instantly draws us into prayer or even leads us into silent adoration before the Lord. When this happens, let us embrace God's grace and give thanks! However, if we commit to *lectio divina* faithfully each day, we may find that such moments don't necessarily happen. This realization helps us to understand the importance of following the path which has been laid out by countless believers before us, throughout the centuries.

Now we follow the path outlined by Guigues the Carthusian, in a text entitled *Lettre sur la vie contemplative* (Letter on a contemplative life). Despite its age, this text remains significant on the subject. Guigues describes a four-step "ladder" that elevates monks "from earth to heaven." These steps include reading, meditation, prayer, and contemplation. To begin our *lectio divina*, we choose a passage of approximately ten verses. We will seek out the guidance of the Holy Spirit, who inspired the Sacred Scriptures, and the intercession of the Virgin Mary, so that she may give us "*an understanding mind to govern thy people*" (1 Kgs 3:9).

Reading

We read the text slowly and attentively, repeating it several times to fully immerse ourselves in it. Speaking the text aloud enhances this process, as it engages three of our senses simultaneously. We can see the words with our eyes, speak them with our mouths, and hear them with our ears. This practice—even if we only do it with a soft whisper—helps us to deeply internalize the Word and bring it into our hearts: "*But the word is very near you; it is in your mouth and in your heart*" (Dt 30:14). Reading it aloud can help us to step out of our thoughts, which often feels more intense than simply "reading silently." Even if we are familiar with the text, we must take a leap of faith each time we read it. Let us trust that the Word of God is always new and that it has something new to reveal to us since the last time we went over it.

Meditation

This versatile word carries multiple meanings. In Psalm 1, we learn that "*Blessed is the man* [whose] *delight is in the law of the Lord, and on his law he meditates day and night*" (1–2). In this context, to meditate means to murmur, to quietly repeat, and to reflect deeply on the Word, allowing it to permeate through our being, transforming both our memory and our heart. We start with one or two verses that resonate deeply within us, "planting them in our hearts" by repeating them in small, manageable sections that don't overwhelm our memory. This practice invites us to engage fully with the Word, focusing all of our attention on it and listening with intention.

We begin by speaking the Word aloud, and then reflecting on it inwardly. Sometimes we are moved to meditate on it deeply, experiencing our hearts being "set ablaze" by God's grace, which is working through those few words.

When we meditate, we can also make connections with other passages in the Bible. A word or an image may remind us of another verse, perhaps in a book from a completely different style or time period. Gradually, we begin to see that God's message is unified throughout the Bible, and is expressed in so many diverse ways. This deepens our understanding of the Word and makes our reading experience both enriching and delightful!

Let us reflect on the Word of God with these questions in mind: What does God want to reveal about himself to me? All of Scripture is given to us so we may see the loving face of our God the Father, and this should guide our meditation. Next, we should ask ourselves: What is the Lord saying to me today? We trust that the Lord wants to speak to each of us in ways that are personal and unique to us.

We can also explore the various layers of meaning in the text: the literal meaning (the text as it was written at that specific moment in time), the Christological meaning (how Jesus fulfills the Word given to Israel), the moral meaning (what the text calls upon us to do), and the eschatological meaning (what has already been achieved in eternal glory).

Prayer

When we carefully read and analyze the text through meditation, we are naturally drawn to prayer—giving praise to the Lord for revealing himself to us, asking him to convert us, to intercede for others, and more. The Word we have received and reflected upon becomes the foundation for the prayers we offer. As the days go by, our prayers deepen, enhanced by the benefits of our meditation. The Lord himself gives us the words to speak to him—not only in the Lord's Prayer and the Psalms but also in other biblical passages and verses.

Contemplation

Sometimes, we are overwhelmed by God's presence during prayer or in one of the steps leading up to it. Let us embrace this as a gift of God's grace and surrender everything else to him.

"Then prayer can be lost in silence; not the silence of absence of the other or of myself, which occurs also at times, but the silence that comes above and beyond the Word when it has affected us."[2] At this point, we can go back one step and freely move between them. These steps may not always follow the same order as is described here; we must align ourselves with the Holy Spirit's guidance, ready to take a pause if he requires it of us.

Which text(s) should you read for your daily *lectio divina?*

The texts of the Mass, which lead us to the very heart of Scripture, are the main priority. Through these texts, we gain a deeper understanding of the liturgical year and unite with believers around the world. All three texts can be read in deep thought, as we take the time to reflect deeply on each of them.

We can then choose a book of the Bible to read in this way, reading it regularly at a speed of around a dozen verses per day.

If you have a bit more time, you can begin your *lectio divina* practice by memorizing parts of the text that are particularly meaningful to you, such as the Sermon on the Mount. Aim for reading two or three

2. Robert Cardinal Sarah with Nicolas Diat, *The Power of Silence: Against the Dictatorship of Noise*, trans. Michael J. Miller (Ignatius Press, 2017), p. 241.

verses a day—not simply to "know them by heart," but to "hold them in your heart." Let the words take root deeply within you.

Conclusion

In conclusion, we thank the Lord for the time spent listening to him. The Word of God has been working within us, even if we can't see the results of this right away. We can take a moment to write down a word or phrase that touched our hearts. As we end our time with *lectio divina*, let us memorize a brief word and carry it in our hearts—so that we can return to this word throughout the day and allow it to dwell within us.

Spiritual exercise

This evening, I reflect on the Word received in the *lectio divina* earlier this morning. How has it supported and guided me today?

. . . .

. . . .

. . . .

. . . .

13

Spiritual Reading

SR. ANNE OF JESUS IDIARTEGARAY

Spiritual reading is a cornerstone of the contemplative life.[1]

—Wilfrid Stinissen

Introduction

In the previous chapters, we discussed how essential and significant the practice of *lectio divina* is. Now we focus on another important subject: spiritual reading. Unlike *lectio divina*, spiritual reading is not limited to Scripture and does not always lead to a time of prayer.

We don't always fully understand how significant this practice is for our spiritual well-being. The demands of daily life often overshadow it, lost amidst the multitude of aspects we feel compelled to juggle in order to keep the delicate and fragile balance of our lives.

1. Wilfrid Stinissen, *Cachés dans l'amour: Manuel de vie carmélitaine* (Carmel, 2011), p. 89. All quotes from this book are our translation.

But this particular aspect of our lives deserves our careful attention, as it plays a significant role in our spiritual journey. Consider the profound impact that certain writings have had on the spiritual paths of many saints. For example, *Confessions* by St. Augustine and Francisco de Osuna's *Third Primer* were pivotal in the conversion of St. Teresa of Ávila. Similarly, *The Imitation of Christ* deeply shaped the heart and life of St. Thérèse of Lisieux, whereas Edith Stein experienced a transformative revelation through reading *The Life of Teresa of Ávila*. The truth is, we cannot be fully satisfied with simply reading and meditating on the Holy Scriptures—although they are central to our Faith. Any spiritual reading that is truly meaningful will inevitably point back to the Scriptures in some way. That being said, there are countless reasons to engage in the practice of spiritual reading. Let us briefly discuss some of these reasons before moving on to the practical aspects of this practice.

Indispensable knowledge

It is common knowledge that it is difficult for us to love that which we don't know—or that which we know poorly. This is true in human relationships but is even more significant when it comes to our relationship with God. Knowledge is the foundation for love, which is why spiritual reading is so essential to our spiritual growth. At its core, this growth involves a deepening of faith, hope, and love. God is both intimately close to us and yet infinitely beyond our understanding. If we do not continually nurture our understanding of him, our love can stagnate, weaken, or fail to mature. However, this isn't about gaining knowledge for its own sake; it's about equipping ourselves to grow in how we live and who we are. As the guidance suggests:

> Read with an open and humble heart, with pure intention, so that you may better understand and fulfill his will. Do not read out of curiosity or a desire to accumulate knowledge for the sake of impressing others.[2]

We should also recognize that God's ways often appear mysterious to us (see Ez 18:25) or, at the very least, difficult to understand (see Is 55:8–11). Although our spiritual journey is not about mastering our relationship with God or fully understanding his infinite wisdom, a basic understanding of spiritual paths can greatly benefit our inner life. Faith cannot grow if we are not informed and enlightened. Therefore, we should not

2. Stinissen, *Cachés dans l'amour,* p. 91.

deprive ourselves of the wisdom that the Church, in her maternal care, provides through the magisterium, the teachings of the saints, or new charisms granted by God to certain individuals—even among our contemporaries—to help illuminate our path. If we humbly and gratefully draw from these treasures offered by God through his Church, this is profoundly enriching and beneficial for us.

The battle of thoughts

Here is another observation. Our intellect is constantly active, or near constantly. Although we can't stop our thoughts, we do have a responsibility over what we "feed" our minds. If what we input into our minds is of high quality—focusing on what we most deeply desire, such as God—we reduce the chances of our minds wandering into thoughts that are useless, unimportant, or even harmful. This can have a profoundly positive impact on our daily lives, particularly during prayer, but also beyond that. When we nurture our desire for God, holiness, steadfast faith, and making Jesus known and loved, we are strengthened and equipped to fight the good fight in faith, instead of getting caught up in trivial or unimportant concerns. As said by Fr. Wilfrid,

> Without regular spiritual reading, it becomes challenging to progress on the path toward God. Any neglect in this area immediately has consequences. Living in God's presence becomes more difficult, and prayer fills with distractions.[3]

During prayer, when we struggle to meditate on the Word or when we feel empty or distracted, it can be helpful to do some spiritual reading so that we can refocus our thoughts on God.

Practical advice

There are two key challenges with spiritual reading: managing our time and choosing the right texts. Managing our time can be a complex challenge.

This largely depends on our living conditions, as well as our temperament and where we currently are in life. That being said, let's explore a few ideas.

Ultimately it's not about the quantity of reading or how long we spend reading. Instead, it's about the quality and depth of your engagement with the texts.

> Do not be satisfied with a quick and superficial reading, but read slowly; give the text the time necessary to enlighten your mind. Pause for a

3. Stinissen, *Cachés dans l'amour,* p. 89.

> moment when something strikes you particularly. Take short breaks to internalize what you have just read.[4]

Even a short reading session can be incredibly beneficial if you are focusing on something that speaks to your current state of mind, inspires your soul, and supports your personal growth. The purpose of spiritual reading isn't to gain knowledge—for knowledge alone can lead to pride. Instead, the purpose is spiritual growth. One common mistake is the temptation to overreach, trying to read too much, or trying to read every good book that you can. But it's not about knowing everything. It's about focusing on what genuinely nurtures your soul. Five minutes of attentive, meaningful reading can be far more beneficial than rushing through stacks of books. When you find a book that truly speaks to your heart, it's easier to make time for reading it, even if you have a busy schedule. Ideally, regularly reading in this way—daily, if possible—will greatly benefit your inner life. If reading every day isn't possible, it's a good idea to make time weekly or monthly that is specifically dedicated to this practice.

When choosing what to read, it's important to focus on what will fit you best at that point—this can

4. Stinissen, *Cachés dans l'amour*, p. 91.

also be explored through spiritual guidance. Over time, you will recognize the unique "coloring" of your soul and draw inspiration from it, even if this means going back to books or authors you have already read extensively. In essence, prioritize quality over quantity. May the Holy Spirit guide each of us in this meaningful practice, and may we support one another by sharing and discussing these choices together from time to time.

Spiritual exercise

This month, I choose a text that will inspire and nurture me.

. . . .

. . . .

. . . .

. . . .

Which readings have had a significant impact on my spiritual journey, and why?

. . . .

. . . .

. . . .

. . . .

14

The Five Spiritual Senses

JOUMANA KHALIL

. . . How could this visitation be more tender, the consolation greater, the light more divine for those hoping, for those sons of light struggling in the darkness of this life, than for the eyes of an enlightened heart somehow, sometimes, in a sudden flash of illuminating grace, to see the one who shows himself, to sense him who promises, to understand that the Lord is mercy and plentiful redemption![1]

—William of Saint-Thierry

1. William of Saint Thierry, *The Mirror of Faith*, trans. Thomas X. Davis (Cistercian, 1979), p. 74, https://archive.org/details/mirroroffaith0000will.

I want to see God!

The desire to see God—or more precisely, to delight in God (*gozar de Dios*)—was what inspired St. Teresa of Ávila, even as a child, to attempt fleeing to the land of the Moors in hopes of dying a martyr's death.[2] Long before her, the bride in the Song of Songs, symbolic of the believing soul, begins her poem with an outcry that could hardly be more "sensual": "*O that you would kiss me with the kisses of your mouth! For your love is better than wine, your anointing oils are fragrant*" (Song 1:2–3). Isn't this longing deeply embedded in every human heart? To see it, to hear it with our own ears, touch it with our hands, embrace it, kiss it, and be enveloped in its divine fragrance, just as Mary Magdalene and the disciples once did:

> That which was from the beginning, which we have heard, which we have seen with our eyes, which we have looked upon and touched with our hands, concerning the word of life . . . that which we have seen and heard we proclaim also to you, so that you may have fellowship with us. (1 Jn 1:1–3)

---

2. See Teresa of Ávila, *The Life of Saint Teresa of Ávila by Herself*, trans. J. M. Cohen (Penguin Classics, 1957), 1.4.

How could this be possible? It is true that God revealed himself through Jesus! The Word became flesh and lived among us. Many were blessed with the opportunity to see him, hear him, be healed by his touch, and be transformed by his gaze. Yet, this was only for a short time. Does this mean that anyone who was not there with Jesus is destined to rely solely on faith without him, as Jesus seemed to suggest to Thomas: "*Blessed are those who have not seen and yet believe*" (Jn 20:29)?

The spiritual senses

The Scriptures invite us to experience the richness of God through language that appeals to the senses:

"*O taste and see that the Lord is good!*" (Ps 34:8), or "*Blessed are the pure in heart, for they shall see God*" (Mt 5:8). In the Book of Revelation, Jesus personally invites us to listen to him: "*If any one hears my voice and opens the door, I will come in to him and eat with him, and he with me*" (Rv 3:20).

Origen, one of the early Fathers of the Church, taught us that in addition to the physical senses, humans possess spiritual senses uniquely attuned to the realm of the divine and immaterial. It is through the eye of the spirit that we perceive God, delight in his presence through contemplation, and are continuously drawn toward him. This perception transcends all reason, allowing us to directly *experience* God in a way that *illuminates* our inner vision, so we can *savor* his sweetness, sense his presence, and *recognize the distinct sound of his voice.*

Developing our spiritual senses

Just as we can develop our physical senses, we are invited by God to develop our spiritual senses so that we can deepen our knowledge and love of God. A child who practices music attunes their ears to become "musical," just as a painter's eye grows more sensitive through education of art and contemplation of creation. Similarly, the more our hearts are engaged when reading and meditating on the Word of God, the better our "spiritual ear" becomes at recognizing the voice of God. Through regular practice of inner silence in prayer, our souls become attuned to discern "God's footsteps" as he walks in the garden of our hearts, allowing us to be touched by his presence and captivated by his fragrance. When prayer becomes a faithful and consistent part of our lives, our inner being is nourished with spiritual sustenance, refining our taste and delight in "divine things." St. Augustine describes this as "fruition"–the "spiritual enjoyment" of the inner senses and the experience of God as "delectable." Likewise, Diadochus of Photice speaks of an overflowing joy when the Holy Spirit enters us: "For when the soul is completely permeated with that ineffable sweetness, at that moment it can think of nothing else, since it rejoices with uninterrupted joy."[3]

St. Ignatius of Loyola's spiritual experience inspired him to introduce a practice in his *Spiritual Exercises* known as "the application of the senses." This involves immersing ourselves fully in meditation on the mysteries of Jesus's life by imagining ourselves as if experiencing the Gospel scenes "in the flesh." The aim of this practice is to bring these moments to life and open ourselves up to God's voice through them. To achieve this, we are encouraged to visualize the people and places, "see" the events unfolding, "hear" the words spoken, "feel" the elements like wind or heat, "sense" the emotions and tensions, and even "touch" Jesus or feel his touch. By engaging deeply with his gentleness,

3. Diadochos of Photiki, *On Spiritual Knowledge and Discrimination: One Hundred Texts*, in *The Philokalia: The Complete Text*, vol. 1, comp. Nikodemos of the Holy Mountain and Makarios of Corinth, trans. G. E. H. Palmer, Philip Sherrard, and Kallistos Ware (Faber, 1979), no. 33, p. 262, https://archive.org/details/philokaliacomple0001unse_k7m6.

manner of speaking, eating, or walking, participants are invited to "feel and taste things inwardly," thus building a profound spiritual connection.

The more that you persist in building an inner focus on God, the more attuned your spiritual senses become. This growth enhances the ability to discern the "voices" that speak to you with greater clarity; in the same way that a child, amidst a thousand sounds, might instinctively recognize the distant jingle of their mother's bracelets–doesn't this bring to mind the memories of the countless times she lifted them up, holding them close to her heart in a loving embrace?

Purification or night

Sometimes though, we may lose our desire for God; his face feels hidden to us, and we can neither hear, nor see, nor sense the presence of God (see Ps 13:1). This experience is similar to what St. John of the Cross refers to as "the night of the senses." It is a crucial step in our soul's growth, as we may become more attached to the experience of God's presence than to God himself. This is a dangerous place to be, and as such an attachment could stop any progress toward the union with God. During the "passive night of the senses," God is the one who purifies the soul, guiding it toward a sense of deeper love. He communicates this not through words or sensory experiences but through the simplicity of contemplation. As the soul emerges from this night, it becomes more humble and open, ready to receive higher enlightenment, spiritual sweetness, and pure love.

The light of the heart

May the Lord have "*the eyes of your hearts enlightened, that you may know what is the hope to which he has called you*" (Eph 1:18). This is his invitation for us to become "a temple for the Holy Spirit" and to recognize his voice, to respond to his divine touch, to rejoice in his presence when we can sense it, and to reflect his fragrance in the world. Our hope is to persevere in love even when God's presence feels distant, to hold on to the belief that his light will break through, and to trust that in the kingdom of God, we will one day behold his radiant light. For "*we shall be like him, for we shall see him as he is*" (1 Jn 3:2).

Spiritual exercise

During my moments of prayer, I ask for the grace to deepen and develop my spiritual senses. I strive to remain focused on what I experience when I am in

God's presence. How does the message of the Gospel resonate within me? Is my heart able to "see" the unseen–is God present in the Host or by my side?

. . . .

. . . .

. . . .

. . . .

I cultivate a deeper silence in prayer to discern his divine touch and invite the experience of his gentleness.

. . . .

. . . .

. . . .

. . . .

15

The Guard of the Heart

JOUMANA KHALIL

Be cautious about isolating yourself and passing judgment on others. Even if you were to reach the pinnacle of perfection, such behavior would undermine the very foundation of your virtues.[1]

—St. Isaac the Syrian

For the Desert Fathers, the heart is the spiritual core of a person, encompassing thoughts, intelligence, discernment, will, wisdom, and judgment. It is also the place of the Spirit and the foundation upon which a spiritual life is built. Therefore, nurturing and safeguarding the heart is regarded as the most essential task in the journey of spiritual growth: *"Keep your heart with all vigilance; for from it flow the springs of life"* (Prv 4:23).

1. Isaac the Syrian, cited in Matta El Meskeen, *L'expérience de Dieu*, p. 173.

What is the guard of your heart?

Nepsis, derived from the Greek word for "vigilance," is a spiritual practice focused on attentively observing everything that occurs within ourselves. It calls us to mindfully guard the heart: "Be the doorkeeper of your heart and allow no thought to enter unexamined."[2] This involves being acutely aware of our internal state, consciously deciding whether to permit our thoughts to take root, whether these are good or harmful. The state of inner peace or turmoil within us is dependent on this practice. This aligns with the discernment of spirits, a concept later developed by St. Ignatius of Loyola. At its core, nepsis aims to build an inner freedom–liberation from destructive passions and invasive thoughts that distract us from God–ultimately leading us to a purity of heart.

What lives in your heart

The psalmist understood that some thoughts are influenced by the enemy and can pull us toward death and emptiness, whereas others are from the Holy Spirit and can lead us into the fullness of life (see Ps 139:23–24). This is why it is essential to reflect on our internal state, much like a garden: What

---

2. Evagrius Ponticus, cited in Antoine Guillaumont, *Un philosophe au désert: Évagre le Pontique* (Libraire Philosophique J. Vrin, 2004), p. 243. Translation ours.

attachments, idols, and addictions take root there? What thoughts are entering? Do they bring tension and conflict or peace, joy, and serenity? When unsettling thoughts appear,[3] they can bring about emotions that, if left unchecked, may lead to anxiety, restlessness, or even impulsive actions.

"It does not lie within our power to decide whether or not these . . . thoughts are going to arise and disturb us. But to dwell on them or not to dwell on them, to excite the passions or not to excite them, does lie within our power."[4] Guarding your heart doesn't mean being disturbed by what you find within it. Instead, it means observing the thoughts and desires that arise in us and consciously deciding whether to embrace them or resist them.

What comes from the outside and what comes from the heart

To guard our hearts and keep them focused on God, we must remain vigilant about the external influences that

3. These may include negative thoughts such as judgments, comparisons, jealousy, envy, hatred, criticism, mockery, or murmuring. These align with what the Desert Fathers referred to as the "eight passionate thoughts," the mental states through which all sins are believed to arise. These include gluttony, lust, greed, anger, sadness, acedia (spiritual sloth), vainglory, and pride. See John of Damascus, "On the Virtues and the Vices," in *The Philokalia*, vol. 2, pp. 334–342, https://ia601006.us.archive.org/18/items/philokaliathecompletetexts/Philokalia%20Volume%202.pdf.

4. John of Damascus, "On the Virtues and the Vices," in *The Philokalia*, vol. 2, p. 337.

subtly shape our thoughts and imagination. Even in the twenty-first century, we can identify certain "wild beasts" lurking at our doorstep: "consumerism, materialism, secularism, the idols of the world of entertainment and sports, and the glut of information."[5] Are we truly aware of what enters our minds through our senses, intellect, and emotions? Although many things may be good, the key lies in discerning what nurtures and safeguards our inner spiritual life and by contrast, what is superficial, invasive, or distracting; that which pulls us away from our love for God, our neighbor, and the practice of continuous prayer.

Guarding the heart also involves being mindful of what comes from it, for Jesus says: "*Not what goes into the mouth defiles a man, but what comes out of the mouth, this defiles a man*" (Mt 15:11). He explains here that what comes out of a person's mouth reflects what is in their heart. Evil thoughts can arise from the heart, making a person unclean (see Mt 18:20).

For those of us who have entrusted our entire lives to God, it is vital to reflect on what comes from our hearts and what is expressed through our words, actions, and demeanor. What do my words reveal about myself?

5. Mother Gail Fitzpatrick, "Enclosure and Solitude of Heart or, Guarding One's Heart," April 26, 2002, International Association of Lay Cistercian Communities, https://cistercianfamily.org/wp-content/uploads/2017/12/Enclosure-and-Solitude-of-Heart-english.pdf.

What does my gaze communicate to those around me, including those who may challenge or upset me? What does my face portray? What does my presence show?

How do I make progress?

Above all, we must remember that this work is indeed possible, *"not by might, nor by power, but by my Spirit, says the Lord of hosts"* (Zec 4:6). Our efforts are vitally important, but without Jesus, we can accomplish nothing (see Jn 15:5). St. Macarius said,

> Man must engage in an inner battle, waging war within his thoughts. The Lord calls on you to confront yourself, to resist and reject evil thoughts rather than indulging in them. Yet, when it comes to fully uprooting sin and the darkness it brings, only divine power has the strength to accomplish this.[6]

That being said, we have a role to play in this fight. But how can we effectively contribute, considering the fact that "nature abhors a vacuum"? Here are a few suggestions:

- When we are faced with thoughts that are judgmental or critical of others, replace them with positive thoughts about the person instead ("Yes, he's late, but he often does small, thoughtful favors without

6. Cited in Matta El Meskeen, *L'expérience de Dieu*, p. 237.

seeking recognition") or consider finding a reason behind it ("Maybe he's not feeling well and didn't get enough sleep").

– Replace judgmental thoughts with lighthearted self-deprecation or humor ("Honestly, it's a good thing I'm around—I'm always right, after all!").

– Instead of mockery, insults, or curses I may have in my heart against someone, I choose to speak a blessing on them instead, such as: "Bless him, Lord, and surround him with your love."

– Ask God for forgiveness by reciting the prayer of the publican and the Jesus Prayer: "Lord Jesus, Son of the living God, have mercy on me, a sinner." This heartfelt prayer lies at the core of the *hesychast* tradition in Eastern monasticism.

Conclusion

Let us never forget that the true guardians of the heart are the habits that we build in a life that is deeply rooted in God: faithful prayer, heartfelt meditation on his Word, daily reflection on our actions to enhance our inner awareness, genuine openness to companionship, compassion, and, most importantly, humility. It is this humility that keeps us from despairing in our daily struggles and compels us to repeatedly turn to God's mercy, which never fails to strengthen us. As Amma Théodora wisely said, "Neither asceticism, nor vigils, nor any form of hardship can save us, but true humility can."[7] This is the humility that we must seek and cultivate in our hearts each day.

When the stakes are high, we must allow "the springs of life" to flow from the heart!

Spiritual exercise

I reflect on my day in the presence of God:

I recognize in my day the source of my growth in love and life, and I am deeply grateful to him for it.

. . . .

. . . .

. . . .

. . . .

I accept the challenges and disappointments that may have appeared in my journey with him. What changes do these experiences encourage me to make in my life? What thoughts have led me to this point? How can

7. Amma Théodora, *Sentences des Mères du Désert*, Pages Orthodoxes la Transfiguration, https://www.pagesorthodoxes.net/saintes-femmes-des-temps-anciens. Translation ours.

I recognize these thoughts earlier, so that I don't let them linger and bring me down?

I place my trust in God without losing heart, asking him for the grace of my ongoing transformation and the protection of my heart.

I look forward to tomorrow, entrusting the people I meet, the situations I face, and the thoughts I have to the Lord.

16

Prayer and Asceticism

FR. JOEL MAISSONNI

. . . To love is to labor to divest and deprive oneself for God of all that is not God.[1]

—St. John of the Cross

The Community of the Beatitudes was inspired by the example of the Carmelite saints, and they view prayer as a "pure dialogue of love" with God.[2] But can this intimate exchange of love exist without asceticism or sacrifice? True love requires us to make space within ourselves for the other person—within our time, our thoughts, and our affections.

Desire opens a space within us, making room inside for us to welcome the other person in. In contrast to this,

1. John of the Cross, *The Ascent of Mount Carmel*, in *Collected Works*, bk. 2, chap. 5, p. 117.

2. Community of the Beatitudes, *Livre de vie* [*Book of life*] (Éditions des Béatitudes, 2021), no. 57.

asceticism (the avoidance of self-indulgence) deepens and preserves this space, keeping it free for God alone. It allows us to clearly recognize that God alone can truly fulfill our emptiness, our longing, and our desire. But what kind of asceticism are we talking about here?

Not all asceticism is Christian

Let us avoid taking a Manichaean approach to asceticism. This perspective views the spirit as being inherently good but trapped within the flesh, which it views as bad. According to this view, asceticism is a means to liberate the spirit from the flesh, allowing us to embrace the spiritual realm.

This perspective is in contrast with the profound mystery of the Incarnation. Through the power of the Holy Spirit, the Word became flesh within Mary's womb. We are called to cherish our flesh as "*a temple of the Holy Spirit*" (1 Cor 6:19) with the same saving love with which "*God so loved the world*" (Jn 3:16).

We must also be cautious of Pelagian asceticism, which professes self-reliance as the way to achieve salvation and reach God. This perspective contradicts the theology of grace, personified in Mary's life. Grace was given to her during the angel Gabriel's annunciation and from the moment of her immaculate conception. In contrast, Christian asceticism helps us to recognize that our human nature—which is good and loved by God, yet wounded by sin—is like a barren land void of water and life, yearning for the life-giving presence of God.

Asceticism of love in view of prayer

It is love that must guide our asceticism in prayer. This is the love for God and for ourselves, for the sake of our salvation. Lord, what can I offer you to express my love, to show that only you can truly fulfill me, my life, and my being? What must I let go of to make room for your grace? My time? My actions? My thoughts? My relationship with technology? My emotions? My body? My comfort? My possessions? My will? My plans? With spiritual guidance, each of us must find the answer according to our state in life, our duties, responsibilities, the promptings of grace, and the stage of spiritual growth we are in. I need to greatly cherish this inner freedom and practice self-denial, so I may fully surrender to the encounter with you. I need to lose everything, to give everything, in order to gain this precious pearl (see Mt 13:43–46). It is the "nothing" of renunciation in view of the "everything" promised by God, as St. John of the Cross teaches.

We will continually need to adjust ourselves to this ascetic practice. There will be times when we can rise joyfully in the middle of the night to worship, times when we need to use sheer willpower just to get up, and also times when we need to show compassion to our weary body and give it the rest it needs. Now is the time to remember that God *"gives to his beloved sleep"* (Ps 127:2), and that the Lord prefers *"mercy, and not sacrifice"* (Mt 9:13). We must never use mercy as an excuse for laziness or complacency. We must also remember that the one who taught us this is the same one who, out of love, offered himself as a sacrifice for our sake.

Asceticism derived from treasure

There is another dimension to the relationship between asceticism and prayer. If the one I adore is truly the Lamb of God—the Lamb sacrificed for the salvation of the world—and if prayer is not merely standing before him but becoming wholly united with him, then prayer compels me to join in this offering for the salvation of the world. This leads me to a different form of asceticism, one often more passive than active, where I move away from self-centeredness, allowing Christ to continue offering himself through me. *"It is no longer I who live, but Christ who lives in me"* (Gal 2:20), and *"in my flesh I complete what is lacking in Christ's afflictions for the sake of his body, that is, the church*" (Col 1:24). This is a good example of the asceticism of St. Thérèse of Lisieux, who, in the darkness of her faith, chose to "sit at the table of sinners" after offering herself as a victim of merciful love. The divine emotional wound in Christ's heart pierces our own hearts with love when we allow ourselves to be united with him. This asceticism requires us to not flee from this wound or seek remedy from it, but to take refuge by entering deeper into the wound of the divine Heart, allowing its love to flow into the world through our own emotional wounds. As St.Thérèse said:

> Living on Love is wiping your Face,
> It's obtaining the pardon of sinners.
> O God of Love! may they return to your grace,
> And may they forever bless your Name.[3]

Asceticism and eschatology

I consider the Immolated Lamb, the sacred Host, this divine heart wounded by love, now glorified in heaven, triumphant over the grave. Prayer binds me inseparably to the Cross and to the glory of heaven. It roots me in a

---

3. Thérèse of Lisieux, "Living on Love," in *The Poetry of St. Thérèse of Lisieux*, stanza 11, p. 11.

form of "painful joy" which is cherished by our Eastern brothers—a paradoxical peace reflected in the words of St. Silouan the Athonite: "Keep thy mind in hell, and despair not."[4] This is the same light that radiates from the transfigured face and body of St. Seraphim of Sarov, deeply marked by trial and by the cross. Asceticism is about embracing the tension between that which has "already" happened and that which has "not yet" happened in the kingdom. We must remain fully engaged with the world through love, while nurturing the longing that grows within us for that final day when "*God may be everything to every one*" (1 Cor 15:28). This is the testimony of St. John the Baptist as he steps aside for Christ, who has now also begun baptizing (see Jn 3:29–30).

It is this charity, inspired by the blessed hope of Our Lord's return, that compels us to lovingly embrace our brothers and sisters, as well as embrace all of creation, building in us a longing for heaven that gradually liberates us from the desires of this world.

---

4. Archimandrite Sophrony, *Saint Silouan the Athonite,* trans. Rosemary Edmonds (St. Vladimir's Seminary Press, 1991), chap. 11.

Spirtual exercise

During my time of prayer, I ask the Lord:
"What must I let go of to make space for love and allow your grace to flow freely?"

. . . .

. . . .

. . . .

. . . .

. . . .

17

Being Docile to the Holy Spirit

SR. MARIE-ELISABETH FOLLIOTT

Natural abilities don't define your worth! True greatness and true abundance lie in being guided and inspired by the Spirit.[1]

—Fr. Marie-Eugène de l'Enfant-Jésus

The gift of God

"The ultimate goal of the Christian life is to attain the Holy Spirit of God"[2]–what a profound and awe-inspiring path! Can this be attained? Yes, but only through the Holy Spirit who makes us "poor in spirit" and guides us toward being truly blessed. Although we

1. Christian Dhavernas, Étienne Michelin, and Christine Verny, *En marche vers Dieu avec le père Marie-Eugène de l'Enfant-Jésus* (Salvator, 2008), p. 42. Translation ours.

2. Seraphim of Sarov, cited in Irina Goraïnoff, *Séraphim de Sarov* (Abbaye de Bellefontaine, 1975), p. 182. Translation ours.

received the Holy Spirit in baptism, we are still called upon to purchase the field where this priceless treasure lies hidden.

The Holy Spirit gives us everything we need: He is the "Lord" and the "giver of life," as we affirm in the Nicene Creed. He reveals the Father to us, makes Christ known to us, and unites God's children with the Father and with one another. The Lord lives within each believer, making them into a temple to him and inspiring their prayer and their praise. Through the Scriptures, he inspired the traditions of the Church, and especially the sacraments, as he continually gives himself to us. As our defender and comforter, he strengthens us in our witness. He is the gift of the Risen Christ, and he brings reconciliation with God and the forgiveness of sins. He unceasingly renews the soul of the Church, adorning it with charisms to build up all believers and to aid with evangelization, a mission in which he is the guiding force. He blesses the faithful with gifts and virtues, transforming them to grow in holiness and radiate the fruits of his presence.

The law of the Spirit

Taking place on the day of *Shavuot*, the feast of the giving of the Torah, this event fulfills the prophecy of Jeremiah (see Jer 31:33); the prophecy of a new law to be written on human hearts. It frees humanity from the law of sin and death (see Rom 8:2), filling individuals with the love of God. This divine love empowers people to live out the high calling of the Sermon on the Mount. God's love is freely given and without compulsion. It draws from and transforms the human soul. His love embodies an inner dynamism that St. Thomas Aquinas describes as the foundational force that moves and directs all actions toward the good.[3]

The works of the flesh

Cardinal Raniero Cantalamessa, preacher of the papal household, often speaks in his homilies of the human struggle to fully embrace God's freely given gift of love and the inspiration it provides to obey the commandment of love as a response to the Beloved. He says, "How does the Spirit give us life? The answer: by making the works of the flesh die! He gives us that life through a death. 'If by the Spirit you put to death the deeds of the body you will live,' St. Paul says in Romans 8:13."[4]

Being docile to the Holy Spirit means embracing

---

3. See Thomas Aquinas, *Summa Theologica,* 1-2.28.

4. Raniero Cantalamessa, OFM Cap., First Advent Sermon 2016–I Believe in the Holy Spirit (December 2, 2016), no. 3, https://www.cantalamessa.org/?p=3158&lang=en.

humility and practicing mortification—a fruit of the Spirit—which Kierkegaard beautifully likens to learning the language of a loved one. The Holy Spirit wants to free us from the confines of our ego, inviting us to cooperate in often subtle ways: restraining ourselves in a moment of impatience, holding back a glance or a word, resisting the urge to scroll through our phones, or faithfully meeting our daily responsibilities. Above all, this cooperation requires a life of humility, obedience to others, and fidelity to the Church. In doing so, we are guided by the Holy Spirit's light, which, as Yves Congar profoundly describes, is both immensely powerful and delicately fragile.

At the school of the Holy Spirit

The *Statutes*[5] of the Community of the Beatitudes invite us to live in the Spirit. Among other things, they emphasize the importance of praying with the people of the first covenant. Within this tradition, we see inspiring examples of obedience to God, such as Simeon: Led by the Spirit in the temple, he prays steadfastly, recognizing and welcoming the Savior into his arms. This shows a profound call upon us

5. See Community of Beatitudes, *Statuts et Directoires 2015*, Statuts Généraux, no. 7, https://www.editions-beatitudes.com/wp-content/uploads/2018/02/x9791030600742.pdf.

to pray and to attentively listen to the Holy Spirit within the "temple" that we ourselves embody. Eastern monasticism is deeply attuned to the Holy Spirit (as seen in the transfiguration of St. Seraphim of Sarov) and echoes this invitation, teaching us the practice of continuous prayer.

The Virgin Mary embraces the Holy Spirit, to whom she was united on the day of the Annunciation. She listens with a receptive heart and responds with obedience, inviting us to join her in her maternal school of faith. Consecration to Mary becomes a privileged path to openness and surrender to the Spirit. Through her, we learn to fix our gaze on Christ. For some, this journey may be deepened by contemplating Mary herself. St. Louis de Montfort encourages us to form a "spiritual image"[6] of Mary, whereas St. Bernard invites us to look to her as the guiding star in moments of danger or temptation,[7] drawing from her light the gifts of peace, love, and the fruits of the Spirit.

The Word of God, when read and meditated upon as Mary did, becomes a place of encounter with the

---

6. See Louis-Marie de Montfort, *The Secret of Mary*, trans. A. P. J. Cruikshank, DD (Art and Book, 1909), p. 33, https://archive.org/details/secretofmaryunve00grig.

7. See Bernard of Clairvaux, "On the '*Missus Est*,'" in *Sermons of St. Bernard on Advent and Christmas*, comp. and trans. St. Mary's Convent, York (Washbourne, 1909), pp. 41–44, https://archive.org/details/sermonsofstberna00bernuoft.

Spirit in its fullest sense. In this sacred space, he speaks, shapes, corrects, strengthens, sends forth (as seen in St. Anthony's calling), consoles, and more. The Word serves as a "safeguard" for our hearts, protecting them from empty words, and it bears fruit in its due season. Rooted within us, it can naturally flow into inspired words and actions. At Cana, Mary recognized what was lacking at the celebration (see Jn 2). Similarly, the Spirit opens our hearts to the needs of others, fosters fraternity, and allows us to live "in genuine relationship"—like him—through dialogue and service rather than self-centeredness. By turning to the Lord and opening ourselves to others, we find the way to truly live through him.

Charisms, in turn, bring tangible expression to this mutual service and the mission of evangelization. Living a charismatic life of humility becomes a valuable way of learning to be open and responsive to the Holy Spirit. Through the Spirit, our lives are no longer our own but belong to him who died and rose again for us (see 2 Cor 5:15).

The practice of thanksgiving and gratitude nurtures this spirit of charity and the "decentering of self." Whether this is before and after a satisfying meal, while gazing upon a beautiful landscape, or reflecting on a completed task, these moments teach us to be open to the guidance of the "All-Loving One," enabling us to entrust everything to him.

Reviewing the day

Reviewing your day can be a sacred moment of reflection: "Holy Spirit, when did you speak to me or visit me today? Was it through Scripture, a person, an event? Did I experience your presence in a task, a service, or a moment of prayer where you moved within me? When did I fail to listen or resist your guidance?" As we acknowledge our shortcomings and seek forgiveness, we open ourselves to a renewed "journey" with the Holy Spirit each day, learning to align ourselves more deeply with the Breath of Life.

Come, Holy Spirit!

From the beginning of Lauds and again at Vespers, the Community of the Beatitudes calls upon the Holy Spirit. He is the one we must desire and call upon throughout the day, so that we may follow him as the early Church did in the Acts of the Apostles. Let us reflect on Peter's remarkable encounter with Cornelius (see Acts 10:23–48). Indeed, focusing on the Holy Spirit allows us to take extraordinary and seemingly impossible steps, as well as to embrace faithfulness in quieter, yet equally inspired and fruitful actions, like those of Simeon and Anna (see Lk 2:22–39).

We are invited to continually seek the guidance of the Holy Spirit, both individually and as a community, as if gathered in a perpetually renewed cenacle, so that he may draw us ever deeper into his divine fervor.

Spiritual exercise

I use this opportunity to reflect on my life by asking myself these questions:

What is the area in which I am most vulnerable, where "the law of the flesh" often holds sway over me, preventing my full expression of life in the Holy Spirit?

. . . .

. . . .

. . . .

. . . .

What unique gift or specific calling has the Lord given to me as a privileged way to "connect" with the Holy Spirit–something that helps me remain in, or rediscover, the grace and freedom to offer myself fully to him?

. . . .

. . . .

. . . .

. . . .

18

Prayer and Action

SR. ANNE OF JESUS

If [you] love . . . a person, then [you will have] a passion that he may love God so as to be loved by Him.[1]

—St. Teresa of Ávila

How can we strike a balance between prayer and action in our daily lives? How do we navigate the seemingly inevitable tension between these two essential sides? How can we give each its rightful place without diminishing the importance of the other? Drawing inspiration from St. Teresa of Ávila—a remarkable contemplative person and an extraordinary woman of action—can offer us profound guidance.

1. Teresa of Ávila, *The Way of Perfection,* chap. 6, par. 9.

Setting the goal

As a wise and attentive teacher, *La Madre* consistently reminds us of the ultimate purpose and foundational principles of the spiritual life. It is essential to point out that the goal of our existence is not simply to excel in prayer or to achieve extraordinary apostolic deeds. Above all else, we must seek out God himself, his presence in our hearts, and the fulfillment of his kingdom of love in the world.

Prayer and action are not opposing realities in competition with each other; instead, they are two complementary facets of a single, essential truth: the practice and pursuit of love. Every prayer and every act of service should be embraced as opportunities to deepen and grow in love. Without this inner drive and motivation, they lose their meaning.

Deprived of the bond that unites them, they risk being perceived as a state of constant separation.

Teresa of Ávila tells us that "both Martha and Mary must entertain our Lord and keep Him as their Guest."[2]

Las obras

"*This* is the end and aim of prayer, my daughters; *this* is the reason of the spiritual marriage whose children

2. Teresa of Ávila, *The Interior Castle*, 3rd ed. trans. the Benedictines of Stanbrook (Thomas Baker, 1921), p. 174, https://ccel.org/ccel/t/teresa/castle2/cache/castle2.pdf.

are always good works. *Works* are the unmistakable sign which shows these favours come from God."[3]

Teresa's message is crystal clear: Prayer is not an end in and of itself. She warned against becoming overly self-absorbed in the joys of prayer, addressing her concerns to sisters she described as "covering their faces."[4] These sisters were more focused on their own spiritual satisfaction than on truly giving of the self. She passionately declared,

> . . . It would be a strange thing, if when God should clearly tell us to do something which regarded Him, we should not do it, but stand gazing upon Him, because we thus pleased ourselves the most! This would indeed be a curious advancement in the love of God: it would be binding His hands, under the idea that there was but *one* way in which He could make us advance.[5]

Let us be clear: If Teresa recommends that we do works in this manner, it is by no means an unreserved praise of the apostolate itself, nor does it diminish the importance of prayer or push it into the background.

According to Teresa, *las obras* encompass all the ways we can lovingly respond to the instructions of God's

3. Teresa of Ávila, *Interior Castle*, p. 172.
4. Teresa of Ávila, *Interior Castle*, p. 83.
5. Teresa of Ávila, *Book of the Foundations*, p. 25.

grace. This includes acts of faith, hope, and charity, as well as our moral conduct. Although apostolic action is certainly a part of this, it is not the only way to express these virtues, and the action must always be rooted in love. Thérèse's central message, then, is a bold declaration that prayer must foster the growth and spread of love. She also emphasizes the importance of living with coherence and integrity in all aspects of our lives.

The same Teresa who testified that "Prayer is the door to those great favours which [God] has bestowed upon me"[6] also confessed that the greatest mistake of her life was abandoning prayer for at least a year. She further affirmed:

> . . . And believe me, it is not length of time which makes a soul advance in prayer, but when being called to other works by obedience and charity, they do these duties well, then . . . the soul advances so much, that in a very short time she is better prepared for enkindling within her the love God, than (wanting these works) she would be by spending many hours in meditation. All must come from [God's] hand.[7]

Thus, in both prayer and action—or more broadly, in all works (*obras*)—our aim should be to respond to the

---

6. Teresa of Ávila, *Life*, chap. 8, par. 9.
7. Teresa of Ávila, *Book of the Foundations*, pp. 31–32.

Lord's love with love of our own, to fulfill his will, and to draw upon his love in prayer so that we can express it in action. At the same time, our actions should inspire a deeper growth in love that enriches our life in prayer. For although the apostolate comes from a life of prayer, it cannot be reduced to that alone. When we live in God and for God, our actions will positively influence and deepen our life in prayer as well.

> "The apostle, through the practice of his ministry, deepens in charity and returns to his private prayer with an even greater love for God. Charity is a unified virtue that grows through acts of love for both God and neighbor." . . . This path to perfection unfolds in a "circular dynamic: from prayer and spiritual exercises to serving one's neighbor, and from this service back to an increasingly profound prayer, all aimed at furthering one's love for neighbor." This cycle "must be continually refined until the two elements–prayer and action–are seamlessly united. This unity represents the ultimate triumph of grace, where human action becomes fully aligned with divine will."[8]

---

8. François-Régis Wilhélem, *Agir dans l'Esprit* (Le Sarment/Fayard, 1998), pp. 324–328. Translation ours.

Humble realism

What can we do as we work toward what we deeply desire: a balance between prayer and action? Apart from setting our goals and allowing the love that unites them to serve as our guide, the answer seems to be found in humble realism. In our daily lives, we must give each of these aspects the attention and space they deserve. But how do we find the proper balance? The benchmark is both simple and universally accessible: one that allows us to fulfill our duties in life.

> The problem of vocation being once settled, and consequently of one's duties of state, any discussion on the value in itself of such or such a way of life is useless—on the excellence of the contemplative life or the active. Vocation places each one in the relative order that it commands and which becomes by that fact the better one for those who are called to it. The acts that it imposes are for those who follow it the most sanctifying. The duties of state that it entails are for them the only way to holiness.
>
> Alas, how many mistakes, how much waste of time and of energy result from false lights on this point, or from errors in perspective.[9]

9. Marie-Eugène de l'Enfant-Jésus. *I Want to See God*, pp. 427–428.

It is essential to give prayer and action their rightful places within our vocation, in keeping with the commitments we have undertaken. We must remain steadfast on this path, avoiding any compromise. We should reduce neither the time and energy devoted to prayer nor the dedication required for our works. All of this must be carried out with humble self-awareness, so that we may recognize our shortcomings and failures for what they are, without claiming them to be virtues or acts of generosity. And above all, we must have the courage to rise again, as often as needed.

In conclusion, despite the tensions and challenges that arise from living a life that is both contemplative and active, we must never lose sight of the beauty and richness of this calling. Let us entrust ourselves to *La Madre*, asking for her intercession and guidance as we follow in the footsteps of the "woman who knew how to love," as beautifully described in Pierre Lauzeral's book. And let us remember this profound truth: "His Majesty bears so tender an affection for us that I cannot doubt He will repay our love for others by augmenting, in a thousand different ways, that which we bear for Him."[10]

10. Teresa of Ávila, *Interior Castle*, pp. 82–83.

Spiritual exercise

I take the time to reflect on the past month in terms of both contemplation and action, aligning this reflection with my responsibilities. If needed, I seek the Lord's guidance and strength to make any necessary adjustments in my life.

. . . .

. . . .

. . . .

. . . .

19

Union with God in Action

GUILLEM FARRE

. . . We praise God with psalms and hymns and spiritual songs while we move our hands in work[–]with the tongue if it possible, and conducive to the edification of the faith,–but if not, then in the heart. . . . We pray moreover that the works of our hands may be directed towards the mark of pleasing God.[1]

—St. Basil the Great

1. Basil the Great, *The Longer Rules*, in *The Ascetic Works of Saint Basil*, trans. W. K. L. Clarke, DD (Society for the Promotion of Christian Knowledge, 1925), p. 206, https://archive.org/details/asceticworksofsa0000basi.

The goodness of action

Poor Martha! She is often seen as the "activist" sister who complains about the "enlightened dreamer." Yet, the Lord commends her sister's approach: "*Mary has chosen the good portion, which shall not be taken away from her*" (Lk 10:42). It is Martha, after all, who reaches out to us most—those of us immersed in a busy life, who are often motivated by a genuine desire to serve Jesus. But can a true union with God be achieved in the midst of action?

Action is a powerful force, and even God himself demonstrates its value from the very beginning. For six days, he created the world, marveling at the goodness of his work. The Sabbath serves as a reminder of this divine activity, which persists even in the stillness of the day of rest: "*My Father is working still, and I am working*" (Jn 5:17).

When God created man and woman, he entrusted them to tend the garden. Work was a blessing, untainted by fatigue or sweat, which came only after the Fall: "*The Lord God took the man and put him in the garden of Eden to till it and keep it*" (Gn 2:15).

We cannot pit action against contemplation, as though one must be endured whereas the other is ideal.

A complex question

Human action, however, is a profoundly intricate subject, one that has captivated the minds of philosophers since ancient times.

Aristotle addressed this topic as early as the fifth century BC in his *Nicomachean Ethics*. His ideas were later taken and expanded upon by Christian theologians during the Middle Ages. Over time, countless thinkers have tried to unravel the mystery of why we feel compelled to create, build, and innovate—this is a profound question that seems to resonate with the essence of our humanity.

Classical authors describe the three aspects of human action: doing, which pertains to material or practical reality; acting, which encompasses ethical or moral ideas; and contemplating, which is entirely inward and reflective. A person's actions ultimately reveal their true character, "*For each tree is known by its own fruit*" (Lk 6:44). Action indeed has an objective dimension, enabling us to create objects and transform the external world. However, it also carries a subjective dimension, through which our outward actions (*ad extra*) can shape and transform us inwardly (*ad intra*).

The inner dimension of action is undeniably significant. In everything we do, we aim for harmony within ourselves, so that we can truly align our desires with our actions, and to act with intention and authenticity. Unfortunately, this is not always the case: "*For I do not do the good I want, but the evil I do not want is what I do,*" laments St. Paul (Rom 7:19). At the core of our actions there is an internal struggle.

However, if the Lord is with us in this struggle, and our union with God becomes the foundation of our very existence, everything changes. When we live in harmony with every dimension of our being—through the work of the Holy Spirit and the fruit of our ongoing conversion—our actions are infused with a force that makes them genuinely effective and positive.

Two benchmarks

To confirm whether our efforts are aligned, we rely on two key benchmarks.

What motivates us to take action? Where are we going when we choose to act? What is the intention behind our efforts? If we remain open and receptive to the inspirations of the Holy Spirit, and if we allow ourselves to be guided by him, our actions become an extension of our relationship with God, and therefore a means of deepening our union with him. This is why it is vital to carefully discern the movements of our hearts. As Fr. Jacques Philippe beautifully writes:

> Where are these inspirations of grace born? Not in our imagination or our head: they well up from the depths of our hearts. To recognize them, therefore, we need to pay attention to what is happening in our hearts, to the "movements" we can perceive there, and learn to discern when those movements come from our nature, from the action of the devil, or from the influence of the Holy Spirit.[2]

This applies to all of our actions, including the most routine tasks, such as work or providing a basic service.

The second benchmark involves reviewing our actions—this is essentially a self-assessment of what we do and how we do it. Since action is inherently dynamic, it is wise to approach it with a mindset of discernment from start to finish, carefully guiding the decisions we make along the way.

Charity must always be the highest guiding principle for our actions, higher than efficiency or any other purely human values. As it is often said, "At the evening of life, we shall be judged on our love."[3] Charity is the greatest

---

2. Jacques Philippe, *In the School of the Holy Spirit*, trans. Helena Scott (Scepter, 2007), p. 40.

3. John of the Cross, *Sayings of Light and Love*, no. 60, as quoted in *Catechism of the Catholic Church*, no. 1022.

virtue, one that will never fade, as St. Paul affirms (see 1 Cor 13:13). Madeleine Delbrêl captures this truth beautifully when she declares:

> Each tiny act is an extraordinary event, in which heaven is given to us, in which we are able to give heaven to others.
>
> It makes no difference what we do, whether we take in hand a broom or a pen. Whether we speak or keep silent. Whether we are sewing or holding a meeting, caring for a sick person or tapping away at the typewriter.
>
> Whatever it is, it's just the outer shell of an amazing inner reality: the soul's encounter, renewed at each moment, in which at each moment, the soul grows in grace and becomes ever more beautiful for her God.
>
> Is the doorbell ringing? Quick, open the door! It's God coming to love us. Is someone asking us to do something? Here you are! . . . it's God coming to love us. Is it time to sit down for lunch? Let's go—it's God coming to love us.
>
> Let's let him.[4]

---

4. Madeleine Delbrêl, *We, the Ordinary People of the Streets*, trans. David Louis Schindler, Jr. and Charles F. Mann (Eerdmans, 2000), Kindle ed., "We, the Ordinary People of the Streets."

Heavenly action

One way or another, action always elicits a response from us. Sometimes, this can be a challenge as it shows us our limitations, difficulties, or failures. At other times, it brings success that fills us with a well-deserved joy and pride. In both situations, we have the opportunity to turn to God—whether in trust and surrender during struggles, or in thanksgiving and gratitude during moments of triumph: *"And whatever you do, in word or deed, do everything in the name of the Lord Jesus, giving thanks to God the Father through him"* (Col 3:17).

In our work, we are called upon to transform the world—this is a calling that resonates deeply with our human nature and leaves no room to ignore it. However, we can only complete this mission meaningfully if we stay rooted in Christ, who is the cornerstone of creation. In him, all that we do finds purpose and direction.

Spiritual exercise

What activity occupies most of my time each day? Which one holds the greatest importance to me? Do I feel a sense of divine purpose in pursuing it?

. . . .

. . . .

. . . .

. . . .

How should I handle challenges, failures, and successes?

. . . .

. . . .

. . . .

. . . .

When I reflect back on my day, what were the intentions driving my actions?

. . . .

. . . .

. . . .

. . . .

20

The Fruitfulness of Prayer

SR. LOUISE DE MARILLAC

As believers we are convinced that prayer is a real force: it opens the world to God. We are convinced that God listens and that he can act in history.[1]

—Pope Benedict XVI

"How great is the power of *Prayer*! One could call it a Queen who has at each instant free access to the King and who is able to obtain whatever she asks."[2] "Ah, if only that were true!" we might think. Yet Thérèse invites us to a deeper faith, challenging us to believe in its reality.

1. Benedict XVI, Interview during the Flight to the Holy Land (May 8, 2009). www.vatican.va.

2. Thérèse of Lisieux, *Story of a Soul: The Autobiography of St. Thérèse of Lisieux*. 3rd ed., trans. John Clarke, OCD (ICS, 1996), p. 271, https://lci-goroka.com/wp-content/uploads/2020/11/saint-therese-of-lisieux-story-of-a-soul-the-autobiography.pdf.

Faith and fruitfulness

Not all of our prayers are answered, but prayer is not about efficiency or automation. Its value goes beyond simply getting answers. Effectiveness and fruitfulness are not the same—fruitfulness is about the deeper essence of life.

The story of Abraham speaks volumes. God calls Abram to leave everything behind, revealing his promise to him. Trusting in God, Abram willingly surrenders everything, embracing his vulnerability and sacrifice. Through his obedience, he enters into a profound and transformative relationship with God. God exclaims: "*No longer shall your name be Abram, but your name shall be Abraham*" (Gn 17:5). Abraham became God's faithful servant, demonstrating complete submission to God's will, even in the most challenging circumstances. The first fruit of Abram's faith was his own transformation—he became Abraham, a true convert. In fulfillment of the divine promise, Abraham was established as the "*father of a multitude*" (Gn 17:5). His fruitfulness is revealed in his role as a father, encompassing his entire being. The same applies to prayer—it starts us on a journey of transformation. God becomes *our* God ("my God"), the God of our days, the God of providence. This bears fruit, whether we recognize it or not, in every season of life (see Jer 17:7–8). Prayer is powerful because it is the time when a trusting and receptive heart meets with God, the One who desires for us to have not only life, but life in abundance (see Jn 10:10). Its fruits are not dependent on our merits, abilities, or even our perfection. As the *Catechism* teaches, the foundation of prayer is humility, born from a deep thirst for God and a recognition of our poverty.[3] Like life-giving medicine for a seriously ill person, prayer connects us—through the act of faith at its core—to the Source of all goodness and life.

A mutual remaining

Jesus says, "*I am the vine, you are the branches. He who abides in me, and I in him, he it is that bears much fruit, for apart from me you can do nothing*" (Jn 15:5). Pope Francis emphasizes that this is a "mutual remaining": "He also remains in us, it is not only we in Him."[4]

Prayer bears fruit for those who pray sincerely from the heart—engaging their whole being at all times, in all places, and in every circumstance. As St. Thérèse of Lisieux beautifully expressed,

---

3. See *Catechism of the Catholic Church*, no. 2559.
4. Francis, Homily (May 13, 2020). www.vatican.va.

> For me, prayer is a surge of the heart, a simple glance toward Heaven, a cry of gratitude and love in the midst of both trial and joy. It is something profound, supernatural, that expands my soul and unites me to Jesus.[5]

Perseverance is essential for those who seek to "abide," and only prayer gives us the strength to do so. Prayer can be likened to a drop of water that nourishes a seed hidden within the earth, whereas God's grace is like the sun, drawing the seed toward light and life, helping it to grow and bear fruit.

The Virgin Mary always remained steadfast in her faith and unwavering in her commitment to the Father's will: "*Behold, I am the handmaid of the Lord; let it be to me according to your word*" (Lk 1:38). Carrying God's promise like a seed planted in fertile soil, she became the mother of all living beings. Faith, above all, is a deeply personal commitment to God. It is also a disposition of the soul and heart, rooted in complete trust in him and surrendering to his divine plans. This trust forms the foundation that sustains the fruit of prayer and helps it to grow.

---

5. Thérèse of Lisieux, Autobiographical Manuscripts, Manuscript C, p. 25, adapted from English translation of transcript at Les Archives du Carmel de Lisieux, https://archives.carmeldelisieux.fr/en/archive/manuscrit-c/.

Intercession

Intercessory prayer, as Pope Francis explains, involves being "a bridge" between God and humanity. Scripture often describes Moses with his "hands outstretched toward God, as if to form with his own person a bridge between heaven and earth." Moses's "faith in God," Francis continues, "is completely at one with the sense of fatherhood he feels toward his people."[6] In the same way, if we want to engage in prayer to a level that reaches the depths of suffering and empathy for others, we must follow Moses's example. Through our faith in God, we are called to stand in solidarity with our brothers and sisters in humanity. Such solidarity requires persevering in prayer—this is prayer that is born of a loving heart and unwavering faith, the kind of prayer that resists the temptations of discouragement and judgment. This steadfastness is what Moses demonstrated when his people fell into sin and turned away from both him and God. Despite his people's failures, Moses remained loyal to them, interceding on their behalf with unwavering faithfulness, as a true servant of God's will (see Ex 32:11–14).

Our prayers are meant to be united with Jesus's great intercessory prayer. When this happens, it becomes

6. Francis, General Audience (June 17, 2020). www.vatican.va.

inherently fruitful, for Jesus has triumphed over sin and death, overcoming every obstacle. Although this truth may be hidden from our earthly perception, through faith we are assured that Christ is victorious and hears every one of our prayers.

Praise

We may not always fully appreciate the transformative power of praise and its profound impact on us. Cardinal Cantalamessa emphasizes this point, stating:

> The greatest miracles of the Holy Spirit are not obtained in response to our supplications, but in response to our praise. . . . The greatest miracle of praise is the one that happens to the one who practices it, especially in trial, because it shows that grace has been stronger than nature.
>
> The miracle of Paul and Silas in the prison—and of the three young men in the furnace—is repeated in multiple circumstances and in endless ways: release from disease, from drug addiction, from a wrongful conviction, from the burden of one's own past.[7]

7. Raniero Cantalamessa, OFM Cap., "Charis' Message in Preparation for Pentecost 2020," *CHARIS*, no. 4 (2020): pp. 12–13, https://charis.international/wp-content/uploads/fourth-issue-charis-magazine-english-1.pdf, p. 13.

Let us try, believe, and stand firm against doubt! Too often, we fail to recognize God's answers, which can sometimes seem paradoxical. However, let us not forget that praise is one of the most powerful and fruitful forms of prayer.

The power of prayer is great, although it often remains hidden from our human perception. Yet, no heartfelt prayer offered in faith ever goes unheard. God inclines his ear to the poor and listens to their cries. He leans toward us and hears our prayers. Undoubtedly, Jesus reminds us—as he did his disciples when their prayers seemed unanswered—that certain victories can only be achieved through prayer and fasting. Thus, we can wholeheartedly embrace this profound affirmation from Thérèse of Lisieux:

> A scholar has said: "*Give me a lever and a fulcrum and I will lift the world.*" What Archimedes was not able to obtain, for his request was not directed by God and was only made from a material viewpoint, the saints have obtained in all its fullness. The Almighty has given them as *fulcrum: HIMSELF ALONE*; as *lever*: PRAYER which burns with a fire of love. And it is in this way that they have *lifted the world*; it is in this way that the saints still militant lift it, and that, until the end of time, the saints to come will lift it.[8]

8. Thérèse of Lisieux, *Story of a Soul*, pp. 288–289.

Spiritual exercise

St. Thérèse stressed the importance of offering thanks to God for his blessings:

> . . . What attracts the most graces from the good God is gratitude, because if we thank him for a benefit, he is touched and hastens to give us ten more and if we let us thank him again with the same effusion, what an incalculable multiplication of graces! I have experienced it, try it and you will see."[9]

Let us try it together and see!

. . . .

. . . .

. . . .

. . . .

---

9. Quoted in Geneviève of the Holy Face, *Advice and Memories from a Novice.*